1. Ice Bean
   (Soy Ice Cream)
2. Soybeans
3. Tempeh
4. Tofu
5. Soybean Burrito
6. Tofu Cheesecake
7. Soymilk

ART, PHOTOGRAPHS and LITHOGRAPHY:
James Hartman, Gregory Lowry, Mark Schlicting, Peter Hoyt, Richard Decker, Paul Heavens, Jane Severson, Kathy Koberstein, Nancy Jones, Jeffery Clark, Valerie Dyess, Thomas Durocher, Bill Brothers, Jody Scheflin, Nancy Boger, Daniel Luna, Brian Hansen, Vance Glavis, Valerie Epstein, Clifford Chappell, Jenny Bryant, Lisa Brinkman, Paul Barnett, David Frohman, Jeanne Kahan, Michele Murchison, Bernice Massey, Edith Lucas, Tobi Lavender, Charles Phillips, Eleanor Dale Evans

RECIPES CONTRIBUTED BY:
Jane Ayers, Janie Baldwin, Elizabeth Barger, Albert, Cynthia and Dorothy Bates, Letitia Coate, Judith Dodge, Barbara Elliott, Marsha Ellis, Mary Felber, Anita Figallo, Edine Frohman, Ina May and Stephen Gaskin, Louise Hagler, Michael Halpin, Maureen Hedrick, Cynthia Holzapfel, Elizabeth Houston, Carol Hoyt, Jane Hunnicutt, Janice Hunger, Karen Jordan, Roberta Kachinsky, Richard Lanham, Judith Lee, Marion Lyon, Cornelia Mandelstein, Ron Maxen, Marna McKinney, Chris Miller, Janet Mundo, Margaret Nofziger, Samuel Piburn, John Pielaszczyk, Laurie Praskin, Carol Pratt, Ellen Schweitzer, Steve and Susan Skinner, Melanie Splendora, Barbara Swain, Patrick Thomas, Ruth Thomas, Serge Torrez, Lani Young

Special thanks to:
Dr. Keith Steinkraus, Dr. C.W. Hesseltine, Dr. Haw Wang, Earl Swain
and to Laurie Praskin, for her editorial contributions to several soyfoods
sections.

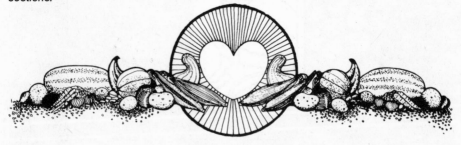

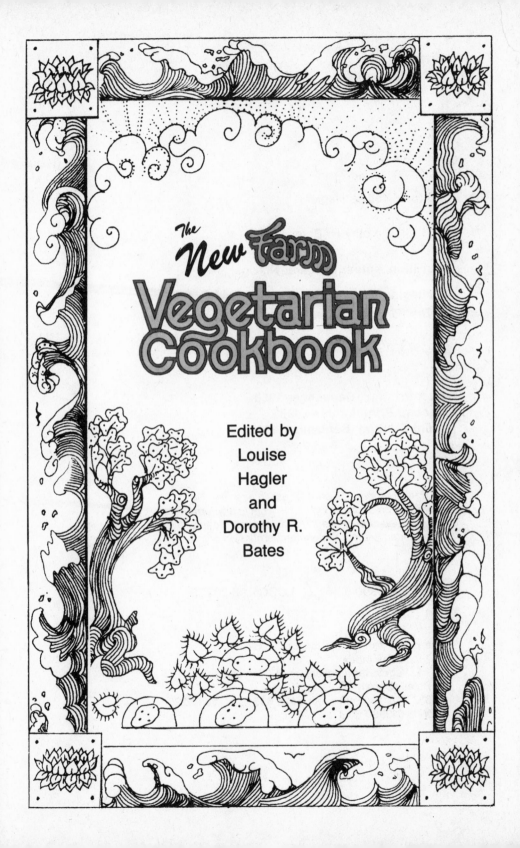

The New Farm Vegetarian Cookbook

Edited by
Louise
Hagler
and
Dorothy R.
Bates

Editors: Louise Hagler

Dorothy R. Bates

Nutrition Notes: Margaret Nofziger

Managing Editor
(The Farm Vegetarian Cookbook, 2nd ed.): Jane Ayers

© 1975, 1978, 1988 Book Publishing Co.

First Printing: September 1988
Second Printing: June 1989
Third Printing: September 1990

ISBN 0-913990-60-4   LCCC# 88-26225

The New Farm vegetarian cookbook
   Includes index
     1. Vegetarian cookery.   I. Hagler Louise.
II. Bates, Dorothy R.
TX837.N48   1988   641.5'636   88-26225
ISBN 0-913990-60-4

INTRODUCTION

It's a far more health conscious world today than it was 10 years ago when we last revised this cookbook. More people are aware that a vegetarian diet promotes longevity and can be varied and delicious. Our palates have been educated to consume less salt, less fat and fewer sweets. Cholesterol is recognized as a menace to health and all of these recipes are cholesterol–free. They were developed over a number of years by good vegetarian cooks at The Farm, an intentional community in Tennessee.

Soybeans are the only legume that can stand alone as a complete protein. Other beans need an accompanying grain to be complete. The useful soybean can be made into milk, tofu, yogurt, sour cream and ice creams. TVP is a dried product made from soybeans that can be rehydrated to use instead of ground meat in recipes. Tempeh, made by a natural culturing of beans, is a highly nutritious and digestible food you can make at home, using tempeh starter. Miso is another product from soybeans, good for flavoring soups and sauces. This book uses soy products, other legumes and vegetables in many creative and tempting ways.

TABLE OF CONTENTS

Buying Your Beans

Soybeans keep well stored in a tightly closed container in a cool, dry place, so you can but them in bulk at a farmer's supply store. One bushel (60 pounds) will feed a family of four for more than a month. **Be sure** *they have not been treated with mercury or other poisonous chemicals.* You want uniform, clean, high quality beans. Untreated beans will germinate if sprouted and soybean sprouts are an excellent source of Vitamin C.

Beans can be bought in bulk at health food stores and coops. Our recipes are based on the commercial oilseed type of soybean, the major one grown in this country. A larger soybean that will cook more quickly may be available but is more expensive. *Always hand-sort all kinds of beans before cooking to be sure there are no small rocks that passed through the seed cleaner. Discard shrivelled beans.*

Cooking Your Beans

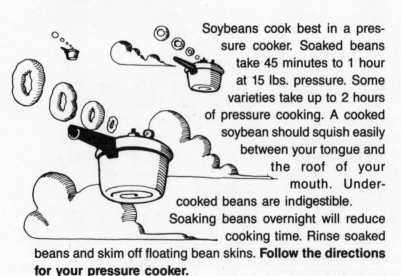

Soybeans cook best in a pressure cooker. Soaked beans take 45 minutes to 1 hour at 15 lbs. pressure. Some varieties take up to 2 hours of pressure cooking. A cooked soybean should squish easily between your tongue and the roof of your mouth. Undercooked beans are indigestible.

Soaking beans overnight will reduce cooking time. Rinse soaked beans and skim off floating bean skins. **Follow the directions for your pressure cooker.**

Basic cooking proportions to follow are: **2 cups of dried beans** to **6 cups of water** and **1 tablespoon of oil.** Oil helps keep loose skins from clogging the steam vent pipe. If the vent pipe become clogged, bring the pressure all the way down, remove the lid, clean out the vent and remove any floating skins. Add a little more oil and return to pressure. Add sàlt to taste after beans are cooked. Soaked beans are less likely to give gas, and cooking the beans with a bay leaf in the kettle prevents gas.

Pinto beans, black beans and **garbanzo beans** should all be soaked and then can be cooked with or without pressure. Cooking time can be reduced if you boil the beans for 2 minutes, then let stand for 1 hour. **Split peas and lentils are best cooked without pressure.**

Keep a variety of dried beans on hand, stored in a cool dry place. One cup of dried beans will make about 2½ to 3 cups of cooked beans. Keep cooked beans refrigerated or frozen.

Cooking times for soaked and/or parboiled beans:		
Legume	Pressure Cooked	No Pressure
Soybeans	45-55 min.	Not Recommended
Pinto beans	45-55 min.	2-2½ hrs.
Garbanzo beans	45-55 min.	2-2½ hrs.
Kidney beans	30-40 min.	2 hrs.
Black beans	35 min.	1 hr.
Great Northerns	10-12 min.	50-60 min.
Navy, Lima beans	10-12 min.	50-60 min.
Black Eyed peas	15 min.	50 -60 min.

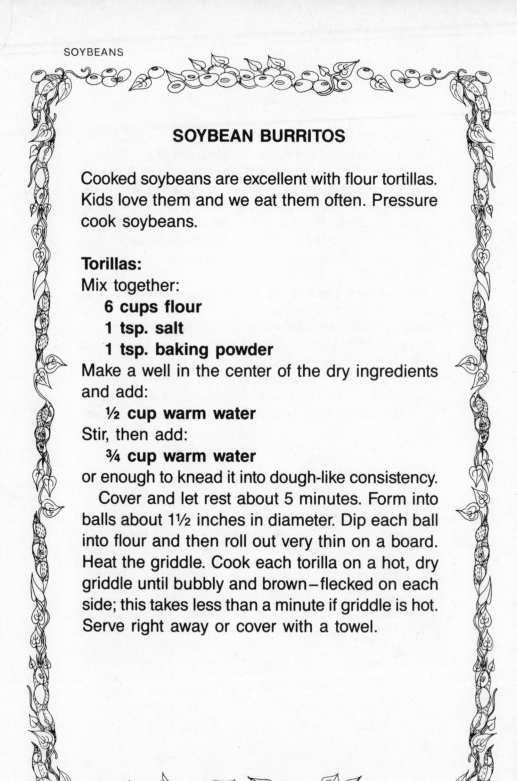

SOYBEAN BURRITOS

Cooked soybeans are excellent with flour tortillas. Kids love them and we eat them often. Pressure cook soybeans.

Torillas:
Mix together:
- **6 cups flour**
- **1 tsp. salt**
- **1 tsp. baking powder**

Make a well in the center of the dry ingredients and add:
- **½ cup warm water**

Stir, then add:
- **¾ cup warm water**

or enough to knead it into dough-like consistency.

Cover and let rest about 5 minutes. Form into balls about 1½ inches in diameter. Dip each ball into flour and then roll out very thin on a board. Heat the griddle. Cook each torilla on a hot, dry griddle until bubbly and brown–flecked on each side; this takes less than a minute if griddle is hot. Serve right away or cover with a towel.

To fix your bean burritos, arrange a line of about ⅓ cup of drained beans across the tortilla. Add hot sauce, salsa or sprinkle with nutritional yeast (see p. 58) and add salt to taste. Roll it up and enjoy.

Soybean burritos make a hit with chopped onions, chopped fresh tomatoes and shredded lettuce rolled up in them.

Nutrition Notes: The protein of soybeans is 100% complete according to the amino acid ratios suggested in *Recommended Dietary Allowances,* 1980, National Academy of Sciences.

☆ See page 58. *Soybean Tortillas*

SOYBURGERS

Makes 16 burgers

Pressure cook **2 cups soybeans.** Drain **5 cups cooked soybeans** through a colander or strainer. Mash the beans with a potato masher and add while mashing:

2 tsp. salt
1 cup uncooked oats or
    1 cup whole wheat flour
½ tsp. pepper
1 Tbsp. garlic powder
2 tsp. oregano
1 tsp. basil
1 onion, finely chopped
1 green pepper, finely chopped (opt.)

Mix well. The batter should be quite stiff. To make patties, roll mix into a small ball, larger than a golf ball but smaller than a tennis ball. Then flatten the ball to ½" thick. Fry in a generous amount of **oil** so they'll be crisp. (Thin patties make better burgers because they stay crisp—thick patties don't get done so well in the middle.)

Serve on *Soft Sandwich Buns* (p.171).

For "Cheeseburgers":

Put a big glob of thick *Melty Nutritional Yeast "Cheese"* (p.59) on your already fried burger and broil for a few minutes.

Soy Fritters with Tofu Tartar Sauce

SOY FRITTERS

Makes 3-3½ dozen

Cook **2 cups dried soybeans,** drain and save the juice. Measure **3 cups cooked beans** and mash.

Combine with the mashed beans:

1½ cups soybean juice
1 cup whole soybeans
2 cups flour
1½ Tbsp. baking powder
1 tsp. salt
1½ tsp. garlic powder
2 medium onions, chopped

The batter will be like a thick paste. Drop by spoonfuls into **hot oil**. Deep fry, turning fritters to get brown on both sides. If the batter doesn't hold shape in hot oil, add more flour.

Serve hot with *Tofu Tartar Sauce (p.134)* or *Tofu Sour Cream (p.134)*.

SOYBEAN STROGANOFF

Cook a pot of **soybeans** and a pot of **rice.** For a sauce, to each cup of *Tofu Salad Dressing* (p.154), blend in:

¾ tsp. garlic powder
1 Tbsp. soy sauce
3 Tbsp. vinegar

Dish up a serving of soybeans over a serving of rice (more than half beans to rice) and enough sauce to wet the two well on top.

Nutrition Notes: ¾ cup cooked soybeans and ¾ cup cooked brown rice give 21.1 gm. of complete protein.

BARBEQUE SOYBEANS

¼ cup oil
3 medium onions
3 cloves garlic, crushed,
  or 1 tsp. garlic powder
1 cup tomato paste
3 cups water
½ cup sugar or ¼ cup honey
1 Tbsp. molasses
2 Tbsp. soy sauce
½ tsp. allspice
1 tsp. salt
1-2 crushed red peppers (about 1-1½ tsp.)
¼ cup vinegar or ½ cup lemon juice
4 cups soybeans, pressure cooked
  and drained

Saute onion and garlic over low flame in oil. Add tomato paste and water and stir well.

Then add, in order, the sugar, molasses, soy sauce, allspice, salt, crushed red peppers, vinegar, and garlic powder (if you don't use whole cloves). Bring to a boil and reduce flame to simmer.

Cook for 15 minutes. Add drained soybeans and stir together. Cook for another 15-20 minutes. It's important to let the soybeans and sauce cook together so that the sauce flavor goes into the beans.

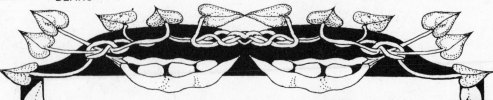

BEATNIK BAKED BEANS

Soak **2 cups pea beans** overnight and cook till tender. Add:

⅓ cup sorghum
1 onion, chopped
1 cup tomatoes, fresh or stewed
1 tsp. salt
1 tsp. dry mustard
1/8 tsp. garlic salt
4 Tbsp. oil

Mix well. Bake in a covered dish for 3 hours in a slow oven. Uncover for last hour.

WHITE BEANS
(Pea Beans or Navy Beans)

2 cups white beans
1 onion, chopped
2 tsp. garlic powder
1 tsp. salt
1/8 bay leaf
½ tsp. basil

Pressure cook the beans for 45 minutes. Saute the chopped onion in a little **oil** until transparent and soft and add to the beans, along with the spices. Simmer about 15 minutes and serve.

CHILI BEAN BURRITOS

Pressure cook **2 cups of pinto** or **kidney beans** for about 1 hour. Bring the pressure down and have ready **2** or **3 chopped onions** and **2 cloves pressed garlic** sauteed together. Add these plus **1 tsp. salt, 2 Tbsp. chili powder** and **2 Tbsp. cumin.** Boil these together for 10-15 minutes.

Fix these burritos the same as *Soybean Burritos* (p.12). You can add chopped raw onions and pour a strip of *Melty Nutritional Yeast "Cheese"* (p.59) alongside the beans.

> **Nutrition Notes:** 1¼ cups cooked pinto beans + 3 tortillas provide 29.4 gm. of protein. 88% of this protein is complete, giving 25.5 gm. of complete protein.

REFRIED BEANS

Cook **2 cups kidney, pinto,** or **black beans** until soft, and mash with a potato masher. In a large frying pan, saute a **large chopped onion** and **2 cloves pressed garlic** in **½ cup oil** until transparent; then add mashed beans, mixing well over heat. Add **salt** to taste and continue cooking until thickened and hot. Serve rolled in tortillas with hot sauce and *Melty Nutritional Yeast "Cheese"* (p.59).

LENTIL LOAF

Cook **1½ cups rinsed lentils** in **3½ cups water until tender.** Partially mash lentils and mix with **2 onions** that have been fried in **¼ cup oil.** Add to lentils and onions:

- **2 cups cooked rice**
- **1 tsp. garlic powder**
- **1 tsp. salt**
- **¼ cup catsup or barbecue sauce**
- **1 tsp. sage**
- **½ tsp. marjoram**

Press into an oiled loaf pan and spread catsup or barbecue sauce on top. Bake at 350° for 1 hour.

DAHL

Cook **2 cups green or yellow split peas** in **6 cups water** with **1 tsp. salt** about 45 minutes until tender and creamy. Fry **2 sliced onions** in **¼ cup oil** until soft. Reduce heat to low, stir in **2 to 3 tsps. curry powder.** Cook a few minutes, add to split peas. Add a dash of **vinegar** and **salt** to taste. Serve over **rice** with *Soy Yogurt* (see p.106).

KIDNEY BEANS
with SOFRITO AMERICANO

Pressure cook **2 cups kidney beans** in **8 cups water** for an hour. Drain and save **1 cup bean juice.**

Saute until golden:

1 medium onion, chopped
1 green pepper, chopped
in **3 Tbsp. oil**

Turn flame to medium low and add:

1 tsp. powdered oregano
1 tsp. ground cumin
1 tsp. garlic powder
1 tsp. chili powder
1 tsp. fresh cilantro, chopped

Saute spices, stirring constantly, for about 3 minutes, but don't burn! Turn flame to medium heat and add:

1 tsp. salt
1 cup tomato sauce
1 cup bean juice
1 tsp. vinegar
1 tsp. sugar
½ bay leaf

Simmer sauce for 5 minutes. Add sauce to beans in pot. Simmer 10-15 minutes until sauce thickens and flavors blend; stir often. Remove bay leaf. Serve over rice.

BLACK BEAN DIP

Pressure cook for 1 hour:
2 cups black beans in
8 cups water

While beans are cooking, saute in small skillet:
2 cups chopped onion in
⅓ cup oil
When onions are soft and slightly browned, turn flame to low and add:
2 tsp. garlic powder
1 tsp. cumin
Stir a few minutes and remove from heat.
When beans are done, drain them, saving liquid. Mash beans well and add:
sauteed onion mixture
¾ cup bean juice
½ tsp. hot sauce
2 tsp. vinegar
1½ tsp. salt
Mash well. Serve with chips or on tortillas.

JALA-PINTO DIP

Pressure cook for 1 hour or until soft:
   2 cups pinto beans in
   8 cups water

Drain beans, reserving ½ cup juice. Saute for 5 minutes:
   ½ cup chopped onion in
   ¼ cup oil

Turn flame to very low and add:
   1½ tsp. garlic powder
   2 tsp. chili powder
   ½ tsp. ground cumin
   ¼ tsp. powdered oregano

Cook a few minutes, stirring constantly. Add ¼ **cup tomato sauce** and fry a few more minutes. Mash beans. Add tomato sauce mixture and mash some more. Add:
   1 tsp. salt
   ½ cup bean juice
   2 tsp. grated raw onion
   2 tsp. pickled jalapeno peppers, chopped
   1 tsp. pickled jalapeno pepper juice

Whip with whisk. Serve with cornchips.

CASHEW TEMPEH SPREAD

4 ounces tempeh, steamed 15 min.
½ cup roasted cashews, chopped
½ cup tofu salad dressing (p.154)
2 Tbsp. soy sauce

Cool tempeh, then grate on coarse side of grater. Roast chopped raw cashews at 350° 10 minutes until lightly browned. Add all ingredients to tempeh with enough salad dressing to get a thick spread. Serve with melba toast or crackers.

GREEN HERB DIP

½ green pepper, cut up
¼ cup onions, cut up
¼ cup parsley, cut up
1 cup tofu
2 Tbsp. oil
2 Tbsp. lemon juice
1 tsp. dill or fresh chopped dill
½ tsp. salt

Puree green pepper, onion and parsley in blender. Add crumbled tofu, oil and lemon juice. Blend in seasonings to taste. Good served with sticks of raw celery, cucumber, carrot or zucchini.

CURRY DIP

1 cup tofu salad dressing (p.154)
2 tsp. curry powder
1 tsp. honey
Make tofu salad dressing with ½ pound tofu.
Stir in curry powder and honey. Let stand to
develop flavor. Serve with **raw vegie sticks:
celery, zucchini, green pepper or cucumber.**

GREEN CHILI DIP

Blend to a creamy consistency:
1 cup tofu
2 Tbsp. lemon juice
2 Tbsp. oil
½ tsp. salt
Add:
1 small can green chilies, chopped
  (do not drain)
Blend again. Chill. Serve with tortilla chips.

OLIVE NUT SPREAD

Blend until smooth:
2 cups tofu
¼ cup oil
¼ cup lemon juice
¼ cup sweet onion, chopped
½ tsp. salt
Stir in:
⅔ cup olives, sliced and stuffed
½ cup walnuts, chopped
Serve with crackers or chips.

TOFU ONION DIP

Blend to a creamy consistency:
 2 cups tofu
 ⅓ cup oil
 ¼ cup vinegar
 2 Tbsp. nutritional yeast flakes ☆ **(opt.)**
 1 Tbsp. sugar or honey
 1 tsp. salt
 1 tsp. garlic powder
 1 tsp. soy sauce
 ½ medium onion, minced
Add a little water or soy milk of it's too thick.

Instant Onion Dip: One package of onion soup mix can be used. Blend tofu, oil and vinegar and omit other ingredients or it will be too salty.

☆ See page 58.

Tofu Onion Dip

PINK DIP

Combine in a blender or processor:
1 cup tofu
2 Tbsp. chopped onion
2 Tbsp. oil
2 Tbsp. vinegar
½ tsp. salt
¼ cup catsup
¼ tsp. curry or cumin
Blend until dip is nice and creamy. For a thinner dip, blend in a little soymilk.

GUACAMOLE

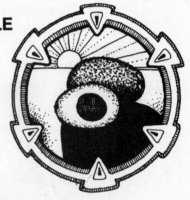

2 or 3 ripe avocados
1 ripe tomato
¼ cup onion, minced
½ tsp. garlic powder
½ tsp. chili powder
2 Tbsp. lemon juice
¾ tsp. salt
Peel and mash the avocados. Peel and chop the tomato. Mix well and serve as a dip with corn chips, as a sandwich filling with sprouts or with refried beans.

Textured vegetable protein is made from soy flour that has had the oil extracted. It is cholesterol free and low in sodium. What remains is mostly protein, fortified with vitamins (including B12) and minerals. It has been cooked under pressure and extruded into small granules or larger chunks.

Dry TVP is rehydrated and cooked to provide texture and protein in many delicious dishes. The granules can be used in any recipe calling for ground meat and the larger chunks are good in stews, fajitas, kebabs or pot pies. It has a long shelf life in the pantry.

Helpful Hints for Cooking
Textured Vegetable Protein

It's really important to add the right amount of water to TVP.

**1 cup dry TVP + 7/8 cup *boiling* water =
2 cups hydrated TVP**

After adding the water, stir until all water is absorbed. Soak for 10 minutes.

When browning, stir often to avoid sticking and burning. When forming the mixture into various shapes, be sure to keep your hands wet. This will keep the mixture from sticking.

TVP TORTILLA AND TACO FILLING

Soak **1½ cups TVP** in **1⅓ cups boiling water** for 10 minutes (turn fire off, do not boil the TVP). Saute **1 medium onion**, chopped, with soaked TVP in **5 Tbsp. vegetable oil**. Season with **salt** and **pepper, chili powder, garlic** and **soy sauce**. This can be added to tortillas as is or added to the following tomato sauce for a juicier taco filling:

Taco Filling Sauce

Simmer together:
2 cups tomato sauce
½ tsp. salt
2 tsp. chili powder
½ tsp. pepper
4 cloves or 2 tsp. garlic powder
1 Tbsp. sugar

Serve the mixture on a white flour tortilla or a taco shell with shredded lettuce, diced onions, and tomatoes.

CHILI DOGS

Makes about 16

Make a half recipe of *Soft Sandwich Bun* dough (p.171) and let rise. Soak **2 cups TVP** in **1¾ cups boiling water** and ½ **tsp. salt** for 10 minutes. Set aside. Chop **1 large onion** and saute in **4 Tbsp. oil.** Add the TVP and saute a few minutes, stirring constantly to prevent burning. Add:

1 cup tomato sauce	**1 cup water**
¾ cup tomato paste	**½ tsp. salt**
1½ tsp. chili powder	**1 tsp. sugar**
½ tsp. garlic powder	**½ tsp. vinegar**
¼ tsp. powdered oregano	**½ tsp. cumin**

Cook this for about 10 minutes over low heat. Divide dough into two parts. Roll one out into a large rectangle 10 x 20 x 1/8". Spread half of the TVP mixture on top.

Cut the dough in half lengthwise. Roll up from both long sides toward the middle so you have 2 long thin rolls. Slice into 3" pieces. Lift with a spatula onto an oiled cookie sheet. Repeat with other half of dough and TVP. Let rise for 10 minutes. Bake at 350° for 20 minutes. Remove and brush with **margarine.** Kids like these—especially dipped in mustard and ketchup.

SLOPPY JOES

Saute **1 large onion**, diced, and **2 medium green peppers**, diced, in **3 Tbsp. oil.**

Add:

1½ cups boiling water	**1 tsp. salt**
2½ cups tomato sauce	**1 Tbsp. soy sauce**
	1 Tbsp. mustard
1-2 Tbsp. chili powder	**1 Tbsp. sugar**
good pinch pepper	**1½ cups dry TVP**

Simmer together for 20 minutes and serve hot over *Soft Sandwich Buns* (p.171).

TVP GRAVY (with Mashed Potatoes)

Have ready: **1 cup TVP** soaked in **7/8 cup boiling water; 3 cups very warm soymilk.**

Saute **1 medium onion**, chopped, in **¼ cup oil** until soft. Remove from heat and mix in **½ cup flour**, then whisk in **⅓ cup cold water** until smooth. Next whisk in soymilk and return to medium heat, stirring occasionally till sauce thickens. Cook 10 minutes more over low heat. Then whisk in the TVP with: **¼ cup nutritional yeast flakes☆ , 1½ tsp. salt, ½ tsp. pepper, 1 tsp. celery seed,** and **2 Tbsp. margarine.** Serve hot over mashed potatoes.

☆ See page 58.

CHILI WITH BEANS
(American Style)

Pressure cook **1¼ cups rinsed and sorted pinto or red kidney beans.**
Soak **1 cup TVP** in **7/8 cup boiling water.** Stir well.

Add **½ tps. garlic powder, ½ tsp. chili powder, 1 tsp. salt.** Stir well, let soak for 10 minutes.

Saute **1 onion,** diced, and **1 clove garlic** in **2 Tbsp. oil.** Add the TVP mixture and brown for a few minutes.

Bring to a boil:
1 cup water
1½ cups tomato sauce
1 cup bean cooking liquid
1–2 Tbsp. chili powder
1 tsp. cumin
1 tsp. salt
1 tsp. sugar (opt.)
pinch of black or red pepper

Add the cooked beans and the TVP mixture to the tomato base and cook for 5 to 10 minutes. Besides TVP, chili is also good with frozen tofu or chopped leftover gluten roast.

SPAGHETTI SAUCE WITH TVP

¼ cup olive oil, margarine, or
  vegetable oil
1 onion
1-2 green peppers
6 cups tomato sauce
3½ tsp. oregano
1½ tsp. sweet basil
½ tsp. allspice
1½ tsp. chili powder (opt.)
½ tsp. hot chili (opt.)
1 bay leaf
¼ heaping tsp. black pepper
1 tsp. salt
1¼ tsp. cumin (opt.)
1½ tsp. garlic powder
1¼ cups TVP

Saute onions and peppers until soft, and then add the tomato sauce and all the spices, except garlic powder, and bring to a boil. Simmer about 20 minutes. Add TVP and garlic powder and let sit for 10 minutes while TVP softens. When TVP is soft, serve on spaghetti noodles with *Spaghetti Balls* (p.35) or cubes of *Deep Fried Tofu* (p.124).

SPAGHETTI BALLS (or Burgers)
Makes 36 spaghetti balls

Soak **2 cups dry TVP** in **1¾ cups boiling water** for 10 minutes. Then add:

1 small onion (diced), sauteed in
2 Tbsp. oil
½ tsp. chili powder   **1 tsp. salt**
½ tsp. garlic powder   **½ tsp. oregano**
pinch of black pepper   **1 Tbsp. soy sauce**

Add **½ cup white flour** and stir until mixed well. Mold this mixture into balls 1" in diameter. Press firmly. Fry in **oil** until crispy. Serve with *Spaghetti Sauce* (p.34) on noodles.

LASAGNE

Makes one 9 x 13" pan

Noodles:

> 2 cups flour
> ½ tsp. salt
> ⅔ cup water

Mix together and knead for 10 minutes. Roll out very thin (about 1/16") and cut into strips 2½-3" wide and the length of the pan you're going to use. Leave them spread out on a tray to dry while you prepare the sauce.

Or, use 1 pound of lasagne noodles, or try *Crepe Noodles* (p.131).

Tomato Sauce:

> 1 **large onion**, chopped
> ¼ **cup oil** or **margarine**
> 5 **cups tomato sauce**
> 2 **tsp. powdered oregano**
> 2 **tsp. chili powder**
> 1 **tsp. basil**
> 1 **tsp. paprika**
> ½ **tsp. allspice**
> 1 **tsp. salt**
> ¼ **tsp. pepper**
> 3 **cloves garlic**, crushed

Saute the chopped onions in oil or margarine until they are transparent. Add remaining ingredients and simmer about 15 minutes, stirring occasionally.

Boil the noodles in **salted water** until tender (about 10 minutes). Drain and rinse in cold water. (If using *Crepe Noodles,* don't boil them—lay them flat in a pan and layer as described below.)

To build lasagne in an oiled baking pan, start with a thin layer of Tomato Sauce, covered with a layer of noodles, next a layer of crumbled **tofu** (p.116). **Salt** this layer, next a layer of Tomato Sauce, then pour a layer of *Melty Nutritional Yeast "Cheese"* (p.59), then repeat, starting with noodles and ending with a generous layer of *Melty "Cheese."*

Bake at 350° for about 35-40 minutes.

EGGPLANT PARMIGAN

Slice an **eggplant** into rounds ½" thick. Place in bowl with **1 tsp. salt** and weight down. Let stand 30 minutes, drain. Dredge with **flour.** Fry in **hot oil** until browned on both sides. Place on baking sheet, top slices with **tomato sauce** and a thin layer of *Melty Nutritional Yeast 'Cheese'* (pg.59). Broil until sauce bubbles and browns. Serve hot.

Pizza Sauce:

1 small onion
3 Tbsp. oil
4 oz. tomato
   paste
1 cup water
¾ tsp. garlic
   powder
1 tsp. oregano
1½ tsp. chili
   powder
2 pinches all-
   spice
1 pinch black
   pepper
½ tsp. basil
small pinch
   cayenne
   (optional)
½ tsp. salt
1 tsp. sugar

Fry the onion in oil until transparent. Add the rest of the ingredients and simmer for about 15 minutes. Makes one cookie sheet size pizza.

Pizza Dough:
- **1 Tbsp. baking yeast**
- **1 tsp. sugar or honey**
- **2 Tbsp. oil**
- **1 cup warm water**
- **3–3½ cups flour**

Sprinkle water over yeast, sugar and oil, let it foam. Mix in flour and knead about 5 minutes, adding more water if needed for a soft, elastic dough. Let rise until double. Oil a cookie sheet and roll dough out on the sheet. Spread with pizza sauce and any toppings: **crumbled tofu,** fresh or frozen, spiced **TVP, soysage patties, fried tempeh pieces,** or **gluten roast.** Garnish with **onion rings, bell pepper slices, fennel seeds, olives** or **mushrooms.** Pour strips of *Melty Nutritional Yeast "Cheese"* (pg.59) over the top. Bake at 425° for 20 to 25 minutes. You can run it under the broiler for a few minutes to slightly brown the "cheese".

CHILI RELLENOS

To prepare **fresh green chilies,** roast about 12 under the broiler or on the griddle, turning them until the skin puffs up all aroumd. Put them immediately in a paper bag, close it, put it on a plate and let sweat for 20 minutes. Then pull off skins and remove the seeds and veins. (Commercially prepared chilies may be used instead.) Fill each pepper either with crumbled, sauteed **tofu** or with thick *Melty Nutritional Yeast "Cheese"*(p.59). Dip each stuffed pepper in a batter of:

1½ cups flour
1 cup water
1 tsp. salt
¼ tsp. pepper

Deep fry in **hot oil** until golden brown. Drain on absorbent paper and serve.

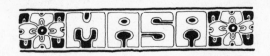

Field corn is the basis of Mexican and Central American cooking. Soaked, boiled for several hours in a solution of water and lime, rinsed and rubbed vigorously to remove the hulls it becomes *Nixtamal,* a soft, shiny yellow corn. It is ground into *masa,* a damp paste, and made into authentic tortillas and tamales. *Masa harina,* or masa flour, can be used with the addition of water.

TORTILLAS

Mix 1¼ **cups of water** and **2 cups masa harina** and knead into a firm, moist lump. Our Central American friends take a small ball of dough in their hands and slap-pat it into a flat, thin round. You can roll a ball out between two sheets of wax paper to an even thickness. This recipe makes 12 6″ tortillas.

Cooking the Tortillas: Place tortilla on a hot, dry griddle. When edges curl up and bubbles appear in the middle, flip and cook the other side (about 1 ½ minutes each side). They will have toasted brown flecks. Tortillas hot off the griddle are good to eat plain, spread with margarine, rolled up with beans or crumbled tofu, adding salsa, onions, and lettuce.

For tacos or tostadas, cook the tortilla in a little oil, then top with beans, seasoned tofu or gluten, salsa and garnishes. Try *TVP Tacos* (p.32).

CORN CHIPS

Cook **tortillas** lightly on one side on a hot, dry griddle. Cut them into quarters and fry in deep **oil** until crispy. Drain on paper towels.

MICHAEL'S TAMALES

Dough:
    4 cups masa harina
    ¼ cup oil
    2½ cups water
    ½ tsp. salt
Knead into a soft, moist dough. Keep covered.

Filling:
    3 Tbsp. oil
    5 cloves garlic, minced
    1 Tbsp. fresh thyme, chopped
    2 Tbsp. fresh parsley, chopped
    1–2 jalapenos, minced
    1 cup tomato puree
    1 Tbsp. salt
    1 tsp. ground cumin
    ½ cup TVP
Saute garlic, thyme and parsley in oil over low heat 5 minutes. Add peppers, puree, salt and cumin. Simmer 5 minutes. Stir in TVP and turn off heat.

Traditional tamales are made with corn husks but you can use canna leaves or small squares of cotton cloth. Fold and steam as you would tamales in corn husks. See diagrams to follow.

To assemble:

Cut the stem of an ear of corn so that the shucks peel off without splitting.

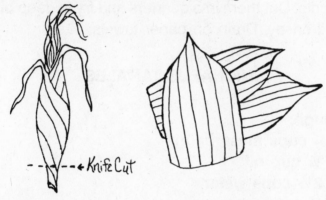

← Knife Cut

Take one wide, long husk or two small ones pasted together with a little tamale dough. Then spread some more dough about 1/8-1/4" thick on the corn husk like this:

1. Place a little filling, which should not be too soupy, but should be juicy, in the middle of the dough. Sprinkle some grated imitation American cheese (optional) over the filling. Fold the right side of the tamale to the center of the dough.

 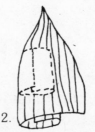

1. 2.

2. Fold the left side over till the left edge of the dough meets the right edge, and press lightly to cause the edges to join. Continue wrapping the left edge of the husk around the tamale.

3. 4.

3. Pinch the ends of the tamale so that the dough closes up the opening at the ends. Fold the top down and the bottom up.

4. Stack the tamales in a basket or on a rack in a pot to keep them out of the water. Stack with flaps down to keep the tamales from unwrapping while cooking. Stack loosely to allow the steam to flow around them. Steam in a covered pot for 1-1½ hours or pressure cook on a rack 40 minutes. When done and slightly cooled, the unwrapped tamale should be tender and nut-like in flavor. It should be firm enough to eat with your fingers.

CORN PUFFS

1 cup masa
1 tsp. baking powder
½ tsp. salt
2 Tbsp. nutritional yeast flakes ☆
1 Tbsp. flour

Mix dry ingredients, knead well into masa. Form the dough into little logs ½" in diameter and 2-3" long. Deep fry and drain.

MASA DUMPLINGS

1 cup masa
½ tsp. baking soda
1 tsp. salt
¼ cup white flour
1 tsp. baking powder
2 Tbsp. sugar (for sweet dumplings only)

Mix dry ingredients, sprinkle onto masa and knead until well mixed. Form into balls 1¼-1½" in diameter and drop a few at a time into plenty of rapidly boiling water. Cook at a good simmer uncovered about 15 minutes. Break one open with a fork to see if it's done. It should be like fresh corn bread inside with a wet layer outside. Serve as part of a main meal, or as a hot dessert with fruit sauce or syrup.   ☆See page 58.

TAMALE PIE

Make cornmeal mush by combining:
  1 cup yellow cornmeal
  1 cup cold water
Whisk into this:
3 cups boiling water
whisking to keep smooth. Then cook mush, covered, in top of a double boiler for 25 minutes, whisking occasionally.

Filling:
  Saute together:
  2 Tbsp. oil
  1 medium onion, chopped
  1 large green pepper, chopped
Add to the pan:
  2 cups fresh or canned tomatoes
  1 Tbsp. chili powder
  2 tsp. cumin
  ½ tsp. garlic powder
  1 tsp. oregano
  1 tsp. salt
Spread half the mush in a casserole dish for the bottom layer.
  Make a layer of:
  2 cups cooked pinto beans
Then cover with the tomato mixture. Spread remaining cornmeal mush on top. Bake at 350° for about 30 minutes. If you make this ahead and it's cold, bake longer until it's bubbly. If you like, add a minced jalapeno to the sauce, frying it with the onions.

ENCHILADAS

Have ready **12–14 masa tortillas** (p.44)
Chili Gravy:
  ¼ cup oil
  1 large onion, chopped fine
  3 cloves garlic, chopped fine, or
    1½ tsp. garlic powder
  1 tsp. cumin
  1 tsp. salt
  3 Tbsp. chili powder
  ⅓ cup flour
  1½ quarts water

Fry onions in oil until soft. Mix in flour and spices, then beat in the water. Simmer 20 minutes, stirring occasionally.

Have ready for filling either:
Cooked Pinto Beans (p.13),
Refried Beans (p.25),
Gluten Roast (p.75), torn in small pieces,
or
Tofu (p.116), flavored how you like it.

Cook tortillas on a hot griddle for a few seconds on each side. Then use tongs to dunk tortilla in the *Chili Gravy* and lay it on a plate. Lay a strip of one of the above mentioned fillings across the tortillas, then roll it up. Cover the bottom of a 9″ x 13″ baking pan with *Chili Gravy* (about 1 cup), line the pan with the rolled tortillas and pour the rest of the gravy over the top. Next pour wide strips of *Melty Nutritional Yeast "Cheese"* (p.59) over the top. Bake at 350° for about 25 minutes.

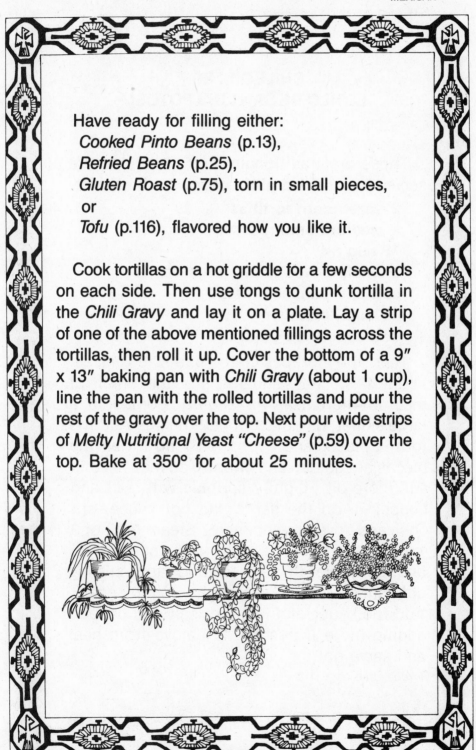

CHILEQUILES
ESTILO DE SAN LUIS POTOSI

Serves 6

These are traditionally quite hot, and are served with **refried pinto beans** for breakfast.

2 dozen corn tortillas
1 medium onion, diced
½ cup oil
3 small cloves garlic, pressed
salt and **pepper** to taste
¾ cup hot sauce
1½ cups fried yuba* (optional)

Tear the tortillas into bite-size pieces, about 1" or 1½" square. Fry the onion at medium-high heat till *slightly* golden in a large skillet, using about half the oil. Add the tortilla pieces and continue frying till all the pieces are golden and crisp. You may need to add more oil. Lightly sprinkle with salt and pepper. Add the garlic and hot sauce, stir once and cover immediately. Steam for 2 or 3 minutes, remove lid. Add remainder of oil and continue to fry, tossing and stirring chilequiles till they are slightly crispy again. Add fried yuba and taste for salt and pepper, adding more if needed. Remove from heat and serve hot.

★*Yuba*–see page 112.

ELLEN'S HOT TOMATO SALSA

Makes 1½-2 quarts

6-8 cups ripe tomatoes, blanched and
   peeled, or **2 cups tomato sauce**
2 cups water
2 cups green or **yellow hot wax peppers**
   or **green chilies** (add a jalapeno
   pepper if you like it *hot*)

¼ cup onions	**1 tsp. garlic powder**
2-3 tsp.salt	**2 Tbsp. vinegar**

Blanch your tomatoes by dipping them in boiling water for 30-60 seconds (depending on tomatoes' ripeness) in a wire basket or cloth bag. Immerse them in cold water and drain. The skins should come off easily. If not, dunk in boiling water again. After peeling off skins, chop in large pieces and put in saucepan.

Finely chop peppers* and onions and add to tomatoes. Add rest of ingredients and bring to a boil. Simmer for about 45 minutes to an hour. Stir occasionally. If the salsa gets too thick while cooking, add more water. The consistency should be juicy. If it's too watery, cook longer. Tomatoes vary on water content.

Hint: Before cutting or working with peppers, oil your hands generously to prevent burning. You can also use rubber or plastic gloves. If you do happen to burn your hands on the pepper juice, take a box of salt and pour generously into both hands. Then gently rub your hands together, making sure you get all parts of the hand.

Sprouts

Sprouting is a nice way to farm and grow vegetables in your own home. It's a simple process requiring about 4-5 days of watering and draining and the result is a highly nutritious vegetable rich in vitamins.

Any seed can be sprouted; it's the first step in the life of any plant. Some of the most common and easiest to grow are alfalfa and mung beans. Most sprouts can be eaten raw in salads, sandwiches, or as side dishes.

Materials:
- Seeds—for best prices, purchase seeds in bulk quantities from a food co-op. *Make sure the seeds have not been treated with mercury or other chemicals.*
- Water.
- Container to grow the spouts in—(a) a glass jar with nylon or cheesecloth stretched across the top and secured with a rubber band, or a piece of wire screen cut to fit inside a mason jar ring; or (b) a tray or cake pan (preferably glass or anything rustproof).
- Colander for rinsing seeds.

Basic Steps:

The steps for growing sprouts are the same for all seeds, although some require a longer growth period than others.

1. Rinse your seeds well, about 3-4 times, to remove bacteria and dust.
2. Soak the seeds overnight in lukewarm to cool water to germinate them. If you're sprouting in a jar, soak them in the same jar.
3. Stretch some nylon or cheesecloth over the top of the jar and secure it with a ring or rubber band.
4. Drain by tilting the jar in a sink. If sprouting on a tray, drain the seeds thoroughly in a colander and spread them on the tray.
5. Sprout the seeds in a warm, dark place. Spread the seeds no more than 2 seeds thick for proper growth. If you're using a jar, turn it sideways and shake the seeds so they line the sides of the jar. If you're using a tray, line the bottom with a damp cloth, spread the seeds, and cover with a cheesecloth.
6. Water the seeds whenever they look dry (usually 2-3 times a day). A spray-mister is a good device to use for watering, especially when growing them on a tray. The seeds in the jar can be rinsed under tap water but should be drained thoroughly.

A full-grown alfalfa sprout should be 1" long. Mung beans should be 1½-2" long. Soybeans should be 1½-2½" long.

If the sprouts start to form tiny leaves at the end of the sprout, they are definitely ready to eat.

Sprouts that are kept dark will be yellow. If they are placed in indirect sunlight for a few hours, they will develop chlorophyll and turn green.

Before serving, submerge the sprouts in cold water and agitate slightly. Most of the seed hulls will float to the top where they can be removed. Drain and serve or store in an airtight container or plastic bag in the refrigerator. They will keep refrigerated for a few days.

Alfalfa Sprouts

LAURIE'S STIR-FRIED VEGETABLES WITH TOFU
(Vegetable Chow-Yuk)

(This is my Grandma Lillian's recipe, updated and made vegetarian with the addition of tofu.)

4 Tbsp. salad oil
3 cups firm tofu, cut into 1½" cubes
1 medium onion, sliced
6 stalks celery, cut into 1" slanted pieces
small bunch green onions, cut in
   half lengthwise
2 large bell peppers, cut into strips
½ cup water
⅓ cup soy sauce
½ tsp. garlic powder
2 cups mung bean sprouts
½ lb. fresh mushrooms, sliced (opt.)

Heat oil in skillet. Add tofu and cook over a medium low heat until the cubes are browned. Stir occasionally to brown all sides of the cubes.

Add vegies (except sprouts and mushrooms), cover and simmer for 5 minutes, stirring several times. Combine water, soy sauce, sugar and garlic. Mix well and pour over tofu and vegies. Continue cooking at a low heat for another 10-15 minutes. During the last 5 minutes add sprouts and mushrooms. Serve over hot rice.

☆ Nutritional Yeast ☆

We eat nutritional yeast regularly for its good quality protein and B vitamins. The kind we use is *Saccharomyces cerevisiae,* a food yeast grown in a molasses solution. This yeast is easily digestible and contains all the essential amino acids. It has a yellow or gold color from its riboflavin content. This yeast contains:

Protein	40%
Fat	1.2%
Carbohydrate	31.5%

B vitamins:
Percentage of U.S.R.D.A. in 2 Tbsp. yeast flakes (9 gm.) or 1 Tbsp. yeast powder (9 gm.):

Thiamin	386%
Riboflavin	337%
Niacin	175%
Vitamin B12	150%
Vitamin B6	270%
Folic Acid	29%

It tastes cheesy in spreads, sauces, salad dressings, crackers, breading meal, and on vegetables and popcorn. Added to soups, gravies and gluten, it has a good, nutty flavor. You can add it to your baby's food, too. Store in a cool, dark place.

This yeast comes in both flakes and powder form. In a recipe calling for flakes, you can use half as much powder.

☆ *Do not* use brewer's yeast or torula yeast in any of these recipes. Use only *Saccharomyces cerevisiae.* It comes in golden or bright yellow flakes or powder. If you use any other kind, these recipes will not taste the same. ☆

MELTY NUTRITIONAL YEAST "CHEESE"

½ cup nutritional yeast flakes
½ cup flour
1 tsp. salt
½ tsp. garlic powder
2 cups water
¼ cup margarine
1 tsp. wet mustard

Mix dry ingredients in a saucepan. Whisk in water. Cook over medium heat, whisking, until it thickens and bubbles. Cook 30 seconds, then remove from heat, whip in margarine and mustard. It will thicken as it cools but will thin when heated, or add water to thin it.

Variation: For a richer, stretchier sauce that's good on pizza, substitute for the flour: **¼ cup cornstarch** and **2 Tbsp. flour.** Instead of margarine, whip in **½ cup of oil** after it cooks, and add as much as **1 cup of water** at the end, or as needed to make a thick, smooth sauce that pours easily. Pour it on pizza and for the last few minutes of baking, put pizza under broiler for a few minutes to form a stretchy, golden brown speckled skin.

CHEEZY CRACKERS

1 cup unbleached white flour
1 cup whole wheat pastry flour
2 tsp. baking powder
½ tsp. salt
½ tsp. garlic powder
1 tsp. chili powder
½ cup nutritional yeast flakes ☆
3 Tbsp. oil
⅔ cup soymilk or water

Mix the dry ingredients, then add oil and milk. Knead into a smooth ball. Preheat oven to 425° and oil two cookie sheets. Divide dough in half, roll out each ball into a thin layer on a cookie sheet. (Or roll out between two sheets of waxed paper.) Sprinkle top with caraway seeds or sesame seeds, if desired, and roll in lightly. Cut into squares, or into diamond shapes. Bake 7 to 10 minutes until golden brown.

☆ See page 58.

YEAST CREPES

Served plain, these are little eggless omelets. Try rolled around ratatouille or filled with mushrooms and topped with tofu sour cream.

2 cups flour
⅓ cup nutritional yeast flakes
½ tsp. baking powder
1 tsp. salt
3 cups soymilk or water
1 Tbsp. oil

Combine all ingredients in blender or beat well by hand. Batter can rest for 30 minutes in the refrigerator. Heat a 9″ skillet and put a few drops of oil on the bottom. Rotate pan to coat bottom. Pour ¼ cup of batter into pan and immeditely tilt and rotate pan so batter forms an even layer over the whole bottom. Cook over medium high heat until the top starts to dry up and edges loosen. Slide pancake turner under the crepe, flip over and cook the other side.

☆ See page 58.

MACARONI AND "CHEESE" CASSEROLE

Serves 5

Cook **3½ cups elbow macaroni.**

In a saucepan, melt **½ cup margarine** over low heat. Beat in **½ cup flour** with a wire whisk and continue to beat over a medium flame until the mixture (called a *roux*) is smooth and bubbly. Whip in **3½ cups boiling water, 1½ tsp. salt, 2 Tbsp. soy sauce, 1½ tsp. garlic powder,** and a **pinch of turmeric,** beating well to dissolve the **roux.**

The sauce should cook until it thickens and bubbles. Then whip in **¼ cup oil** and **1 cup nutritional yeast flakes** ☆.

Mix part of the sauce with the noodles and put in casserole dish, and pour a generous amount of sauce on top. Sprinkle top with **paprika** and bake for 15 minutes in a 350° preheated oven. Put in broiler for a few minutes until "cheese" sauce gets stretchy and crisp.

☆ See page 58.

BUCKWHEAT GROATS
AND GOLDEN GRAVY

Groats:

Buy toasted groats (kasha), or roast groats on a cookie sheet at 350° for about 10 minutes until browned. To **1½ cups groats** add **3 cups boiling water.** Cover and cook over low heat 15 to 20 minutes until water is absorbed; don't stir. Serve as a cereal or a main meal with *Golden Gravy.*

Golden Gravy:

⅓ cup white unbleached flour
⅓ cup nutritional yeast flakes ☆
¼ cup oil or margarine
2 cups water
1 Tbsp. soy sauce

Toast the flour over medium low heat until you can start to smell it. Stir in the yeast, then add oil. Cook a few minutes until bubbly, then add water and cook, whisking until it thickens and bubbles. Add soy sauce, and add salt and pepper to taste.

☆ See page 58.

Varnishkas:

While kasha is cooking, fry **l large onion,** chopped, in **2 Tbsp. oil.** Cook and drain **12 oz. package of "bow ties" pasta.** Mix fried onions, kasha and pasta, add salt and pepper to taste.

UNCLE BILL

We feel blessed to have had Uncle Bill live with us the last few years of his life. Born in Poland, brought up in Brooklyn, he spent much of his life as a delicatessen manager in New York City.

Uncle Bill came to us from a nursing home in Florida when he was 81. At first he wasn't used to our diet, but soon he was cooking Jewish dishes vegetarian style. You would find him in a Farm kitchen mixing, seasoning and tasting. He loved parties and kids. He taught us a lot about good food, and he taught us that old folks are a groove to have around. We will always remember Uncle Bill with love.

ONION ROLLS

2 medium onions,	**⅓ tsp. salt**
chopped fine	**⅓ tsp. dill**
⅓ cup oil	**⅓ tsp. garlic**
	1/8 tsp. pepper

Saute onions in oil until golden brown. Add spices and fry another minute. Remove from heat. Using *Soft Sandwich Buns* recipe (p.171), make rolls and put on trays. Cover the top of each roll with 1 tsp. of sauteed onion mixture before they rise. Let rolls rise ½ hour and bake at 375° for 20 minutes or until the bottoms are brown and the tops are beginning to brown.

PICKLED "LOX"

Slice **1 medium eggplant** into pieces approximately 2" long, 1" wide, and ¼" thick. Place in a bowl and cover with **salt**. Press with a weight overnight. Drain the water off in the morning. Fry in **⅓ cup oil** until soft but not mushy. Add **2 Tbsp. vinegar, 1 tsp. garlic powder,** and **¼ tsp. pepper.** Fry another minute. Let cool. Serve on bagels with *Yogurt Cream Cheese* (p.110).

PICKLED "HERRING"

Take the cooled *Pickled "Lox"* and add **1½ cups** *Tofu Sour Cream* (p.136), **1 onion** sliced very fine, and **1 Tbsp. lemon juice.**

KNISHES

Dough:
Combine:

1 cup cooked potatoes, peeled and mashed

¼ cup oil

1 tsp. salt

Add:

3 cups flour, mixed with

1 tsp. baking powder

Mix well. Make a well in the center of the flour mixture and add **½ cup cold water.** Knead into a smooth dough. Let rest on a lightly floured board and cover with a bowl or cloth for ½ hour.

Cut dough into 4 sections. Roll as thin as possible. Cut into rectangles about 2 x 3" for regular knishes or smaller for appetizers. Place filling in center of rectangle and fold the two shorter ends toward the center first. Then fold the two longer ends over each other. Bake on a well-oiled baking sheet, fold side down, till golden, about ½ hour in a 350° oven.

Potato Filling:

Combine and mix well:

1½ **cups mashed potatoes**
½ **tsp. salt**
¼ **tsp. pepper**
½ **cup onions,** sauteed in
¼ **cup margarine**

Buckwheat Filling:

Combine **1½ cups kasha,** or **roasted groats,** with **3 cups boiling water, 1 tsp. salt.** Cook over low heat until water is absorbed, 15 to 20 minutes. Fry **2 medium onions,** chopped, in ½ **cup oil.** Mix.

SOUPS

ELLEN'S GOOD FOR YA
NOODLE SOUP

Serves 12

2 medium onions

5 Tbsp. oil

6 quarts water

1 cup green split peas

4 bay leaves

1½ tsp. celery seed

1 tsp. salt

⅓ tsp. pepper

4 Tbsp. soy sauce

5-6 cups spaghetti, broken into small pieces

4 Tbsp. nutritional yeast flakes ☆

4-5½ cups more water

Chop the onions, then saute in oil until medium brown. Set aside. Bring water to a boil and add split peas, bay leaves, and celery seed. With lid on, cook the peas until they dissolve and make a light green broth (one hour or so). Then add salt, pepper, soy sauce and onions (scrape the oil they're in and put in soup, too). You will probably have to add the 4-5½ cups more water during the course

of cooking the peas because they boil down a lot. Keep the soup boiling lightly and add the noodles. Cook until tender. Whisk in nutritional yeast.

ONION SOUP

Serves 6

5 cups onions,	**2 tsp. salt**
sliced in rings	**1/8 tsp. pepper**
5 Tbsp. oil	**3-4 Tbsp. soy sauce**
7½ cups water	**3 Tbsp. nutritional**
2½ tsp. tarragon	**yeast flakes ☆**

Fry onions in oil in a cast iron skillet until they're well browned. Meanwhile, put water on to boil. Add onions, tarragon, salt and pepper to boiling water and turn down to simmer slowly for 5-10 minutes.

Add soy sauce and yeast at the end. You can make a lot of this soup and refrigerate it overnight. Sitting overnight enhances the flavor.

☆ See page 58.

MINESTRONE SOUP

Pressure cook **2 cups kidney beans** for 1 hour or until soft. Then saute:

2 onions, chopped
4 stalks of celery, chopped
4 carrots, cut in rounds
1 small cabbage, shredded

in ½ **cup oil** until limp. If you are going to add potatoes, add them at this time also.

Next add:
4 cups stewed tomatoes
2 tsp. garlic powder
2 tsp. oregano
4 tsp. basil
1 Tbsp. salt
½ tsp. pepper
1 Tbsp. dried parsley
8 cups water

When this comes to a boil, add **1 cup noodles** or **cooked rice.**

Boil for 15 minutes, stirring occasionally to keep from sticking. Add the beans and simmer for a few minutes before serving.

PESTO

4-5 cloves garlic
2 Tbsp. dried basil
¼-½ cup oil

Mince garlic very fine or use garlic press. Add basil, then oil, and mix together, rubbing garlic and basil against side of cup so as to get the juices into the oil.

Add to *Minestrone* or pasta before serving.

ROBERTA'S GOOD SOUP

Saute **1 medium onion** (diced) in **3 Tbsp. oil**. Add the onion to:

5 cups boiling water
1 tsp. salt
1/8 tsp. black pepper
¼ tsp. celery seed
¼ cup dry TVP
1 tsp. soy sauce

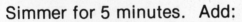

Simmer for 5 minutes. Add:

½ cup nutritional yeast flakes ☆
1½ Tbsp. margarine
2 cups cooked noodles
   or **1-1½ cups cooked rice**

This is a quick and easy soup to make and kids love it. Serve with sprouts and/or crackers.

☆ See page 58.

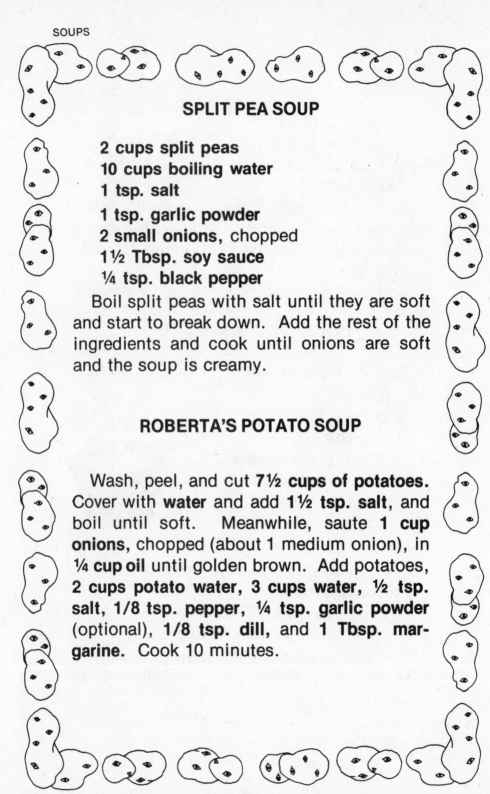

SPLIT PEA SOUP

2 cups split peas
10 cups boiling water
1 tsp. salt
1 tsp. garlic powder
2 small onions, chopped
1½ Tbsp. soy sauce
¼ tsp. black pepper

Boil split peas with salt until they are soft and start to break down. Add the rest of the ingredients and cook until onions are soft and the soup is creamy.

ROBERTA'S POTATO SOUP

Wash, peel, and cut 7½ cups of potatoes. Cover with water and add 1½ tsp. salt, and boil until soft. Meanwhile, saute 1 cup onions, chopped (about 1 medium onion), in ¼ cup oil until golden brown. Add potatoes, 2 cups potato water, 3 cups water, ½ tsp. salt, 1/8 tsp. pepper, ¼ tsp. garlic powder (optional), 1/8 tsp. dill, and 1 Tbsp. margarine. Cook 10 minutes.

CREAM OF POTATO SOUP

Scrub and cut **10 cups white potatoes.** Boil until soft in **6 cups water** and **2 tsp. salt.**

Meanwhile, saute **1 medium onion** (about 1-1½ cups) in **¼ cup oil.** Add **¼ cup flour** to onions to make a smooth paste. Stir constantly.

Drain potatoes, saving the water. Mash **2 cups potatoes** and add to potatoes in pot, along with:

4 cups potato water
2 cups soymilk
onion-flour paste
1½ tsp. salt
¼ tsp. pepper
¼ tsp. dill weed
1 Tbsp. margarine

Cook over low heat 10-15 minutes.

"To feed yourself may even be a sin—it depends on how overweight you are. But to feed someone else is a Holy duty."
—Rabbi Shlomo Carlbach

GLUTEN

Gluten is the protein in wheat that holds bread together. Making gluten is a process of kneading flour and water into a dough, soaking it in water and kneading it several times until the starch is removed from the flour. After cooking, gluten has a chewy, elastic texture like meat and with the addition of oil and seasonings makes delicious, nutritious food. It has the things you liked about meat without taking the life of an animal.

BASIC RAW GLUTEN

8 cups wheat flour (half unbleached white or whole–wheat and half gluten flour)
2–3 cups water (or enough for a stiff dough)
Knead 10 to 15 minutes until you have a smooth, elastic ball of dough. It should spring back when poked. Put in a large bowl, cover with water. Let soak an hour. Knead it under water, kneading out the starch and holding gluten together. Change water when it gets milky. Let it rest. Repeat the process of kneading, changing the water and letting it rest several times. When water stays almost clear, you will have 4 to 5 cups of raw gluten ready to be spice, oiled and cooked.

Chunks can be simmered in a savory broth (add soy sauce, onion, oil to vegetable stock, simmer about an hour and thicken liquid for gravy). It can be baked for a roast or pot roast, oven–fried or cooked in barbeque sauce.

Leftover cooked gluten is good sliced for sandwiches, chopped bite–size and added to chili or used on pizza.

GLUTEN ROAST

Have **4 cups raw gluten** ready.
Combine in a bowl:

½ cup oil
3 Tbsp. soy sauce
1 tsp. salt
¼ cup peanut butter or tahini (opt.)
1 cup warm water
1 tsp. garlic powder
1 tsp. onion powder
¼ tsp. black pepper

Work the seasonings into the raw gluten, some sauce will remain. Shape gluten into an oiled loaf pan. Add **2 cups of water** to remaining sauce. If no sauce is left, add **2 Tbsp. soy sauce** and **2 Tbsp. oil** to water. Pour over loaf. Place **2 onions** in thick slices on top. Sauce should come almost to top of loaf; if not add a little more water. Cover tightly with foil. Bake at 350° for 1 to 1½ hours. Uncover for last 15 minutes of baking, baste. Liquid left in pan can be thickened for gravy.

Gluten Pot Roast: Follow the directions for *Gluten Roast,* but use a Dutch oven or roasting pan instead of a loaf pan. Around the roast place **potatoes, carrots** and **onions.** Cover roast with: **¼ cup oil, ¼ cup soy sauce** and **1 cup water.**

Bake at 350° uncovered for the first half hour, then covered for half an hour and then uncovered again for the last half hour. Baste several times.

OVEN FRIED GLUTEN

Have ready **3–4 cups washed raw gluten.**
Cook until tender:
  1 large onion, chopped very fine
  3 cloves garlic, minced
  ¼ cup oil
When onions are soft, add seasonings:
  ½ tsp. marjoram
  ½ tsp. thyme
  ½ tsp. sage
  ¼ cup nutritional yeast flakes ☆
  1 tsp. salt
  1 Tbsp. soy sauce
  2 Tbsp. peanut butter (opt.)
Work onions and seasoning into gluten with your fingers. Pull off pieces and stretch flat, 4" long and about 2" wide, less than ½" thick. Roll each piece in crumb mixture. Place on a well–oiled cookie sheet. Makes 15 to 20 pieces.

Crumb Mixture:
  1¾ cups bread or cracker crumbs
  ¼ cup wheat germ
  1 tsp. garlic powder
  2 Tbsp. nutritional yeast flakes ☆
  ½ tsp. salt
  ½ tsp. paprika
  ¼ tsp. pepper or thyme
Bake at 350° for 15 minutes, turn pieces over. Bake 15 to 20 minutes more until golden brown. Don't overbake.

☆See page 58.

SUSAN'S GLUTEN STEAKS

3 dozen pieces

Mix in a large bowl:
6 cups unbleached bread flour
4 cups instant gluten flour
Measure into another bowl:
4½ cups water
Whisk the flour mixture into the water 2 cups at a time. Knead into a smooth dough, keeping it together about 10 to 15 minutes. Shape into a ball and cover with cold water. Let stand for 1 hour. Knead the gluten, squeezing it through your fingers without tearing it into small pieces. Change water when it becomes very milky. Repeat this kneading and water changing 4 or 5 times. During the last rinse, pull the dough through your fingers to make it stringy, shaping it into long thin "steaks" or "ribs".

Coat gluten with a mixture of:
½ cup margarine
1 large onion, chopped
½ cup nutritional yeast ☆
½ cup tahini or peanut butter
1 Tbsp. salt
½ cup barbeque sauce
Preheat oven to 350°. Place gluten pieces on a well-oiled cookie sheet. Bake 15 minutes, then coat with any barbeque sauce. Turn over, top with sauce. Reduce heat to 300° and bake 15 to 20 minutes more.

JANICE'S
BARBEQUE GLUTEN "RIBS"

4 cups washed gluten
⅓ cup nutritional yeast flakes☆
2 Tbsp. peanut butter
1 Tbsp. paprika
1 Tbsp. salt, or to taste
1 large onion, chopped and sauteed in
½ cup oil

Put gluten in bowl with nutritional yeast, peanut butter, paprika and salt on top. Pour hot sauteed onions and margarine over all. While everything is still warm, mix well with hands until the gluten is in stringy, chunky pieces. The hot margarine breaks the gluten down and helps the seasonings penetrate.

Break the gluten off in good-sized pieces to make 2 x 4" gluten "ribs" by pulling, twisting and flattening them to about ¼-½" thick. Do not roll out or cut, as this makes the gluten like bread instead of being chewy.

Pour ¼-½ **cup oil** onto large cookie sheet. Place "ribs" of gluten on sheet and bake in a 350-400° oven for 1 hour or until very crispy and brown on bottom. Pour about **2 cups** *Barbeque Sauce* (see next page) per sheet over gluten and bake 10 minutes longer.

☆ See page 58.

BARBEQUE SAUCE

makes 3 cups

1 large onion, chopped
2 cloves garlic, minced
¼ cup oil
2½ cups tomato sauce
¼ cup water
½ cup brown sugar
1 Tbsp. molasses
½ cup mustard
1 tsp. salt
1 tsp. allspice
2 tsp. crushed red pepper
2 Tbsp. parsley, minced
¼ cup water
1 Tbsp. soy sauce
¼ cup lemon juice

Saute chopped onion and minced garlic in oil until onions are soft. Use a heavy bottomed pan. Add all ingredients except lemon juice and soy sauce. Bring to a boil, reduce heat, cover and simmer for an hour. Stir occasionally. Add lemon juice and soy sauce and cook 10 minutes longer. This keeps well in refrigerator.

GLUTEN BURRITOS

Fry left-over **roasted gluten** with **chopped onions, chopped tomatoes,** and a little **chili.** Fold into large **flour tortillas** (p.12).

Tempeh

Tempeh is a delicious, high-protein main dish made from soybeans. It has been a staple in Indonesia for centuries. Like cheese, yogurt, and sourdough, tempeh is made by natural culturing; the soybeans are cultured with a mold called *Rhizopus oligosporus*. This form of soybeans contains more riboflavin, niacin, and B6 than unfermented soybeans. The protein in tempeh is partially broken down during fermentation, which makes it highly digestible. Children love it, and its ease of digestion makes it particularly suitable for older folks.

Tempeh is easily made at home with basic kitchen supplies. Lightly cooked, split, hulled soybeans are mixed with tempeh starter and allowed to stand in a warm place overnight. The white cake which forms is a quick-cooking, pleasant-tasting, high-protein food that can be prepared in a variety of ways.

MAKING TEMPEH AT HOME

Yield: 10-12 pieces, 4 x 3 x ½"

Materials You'll Need

Ingredients:

2½ **cups dry soybeans,** split and hulled*

1 **tsp. tempeh starter**

2 **Tbsp. vinegar**

*You can split them in a hand grain mill. As they cook the hulls float up and can be skimmed off. Or, see *Other Methods for Splitting and Hulling Whole Soybeans* on page 86.

Tempeh Containers:

The containers should allow enough air to get in so the tempeh can grow, but not so much that the beans dry out. They should hold and maintain the humidity of the fermenting mass, without drowning the mold.

- **Cake pan:** Stretch a piece of tin foil over the top and punch holes in the foil every inch or so.
- **Plastic bag:** Punch holes on both sides about every inch with a fork. Put in a ½" layer of beans. Place bag on a wire cooling rack so air reaches both sides.

Preparation:

1. Cook the split soybeans for 1½ hours at a bubbling boil, skimming off any bean skins that float to the top. (If some are left, that's okay.)
2. Drain off excess moisture, then knead the beans in a towel until they are surface dry. Put the beans in a dry bowl. Having the beans too wet is the most common cause of a bad batch.
3. When they are cooler than skin temperature, add the vinegar and mix well. Then add the starter and mix very well. (Refrigerate starter package in a closed container.)

4. Firmly pack a ½" deep layer of beans into tempeh container.

Growing the Tempeh:

Set the container in a warm place with a stable 85-95° temperature. 90° is best. Check the temperature occasionally. A sunny window or attic, a high kitchen shelf, or a closet with a drop light are some good incubation places. Don't incubate in a small airtight box, as the mold needs oxygen.

For the first 12 hours, the mold is getting started. At 12-15 hours, water condenses on the cover of the tempeh containers and the white mold begins to show faintly on the beans. The tempeh is now producing heat, so check the temperature and adjust it if necessary.

Almost ready

After 19-23 hours, the tempeh looks like white icing on a cake. In the next 2-3 hours, gray or black spots begin to show, especially around the holes in the container. Gray or black areas are the natural result of sporulation (when the mold forms its "seeds") and are not harmful.

In the last 2-3 hours of the 19-26 hour period, the tempeh gets most of its flavor, so be sure to let it grow long enough.

Checking the Tempeh:

Good Tempeh—The beans are solidly bound into a white cake marbled with gray or black. If it's black all over, it has just incubated too long; it's still good to eat unless it smells strongly of ammonia. Fresh tempeh smells good, like bread dough or fresh mushrooms. It may smell faintly of ammonia. A thin slice of tempeh holds together without crumbling. The mold completely fills the spaces between the beans. Good tempeh smells good and feels solid on the bottom.

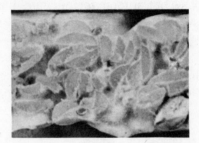

A slice of good tempeh looks like this   *Unfinished tempeh looks like this*

Unfinished Tempeh—The mold is usually pure white with no gray areas. The beans are bound together loosely and the mold doesn't fill the spaces between the beans. It crumbles when sliced. Unfinished tempeh doesn't have much flavor when cooked and the beans are a little crunchy. Uneven heat distribution may cause part of the batch to finish late. If this occurs, cut off the finished part and let the rest go longer.

Inedible Tempeh—It smells unpleasant or strongly of ammonia. It may be sticky or slimy all over or in spots. The mold may grow only in patches or not at all. Or it may be well-molded on top, but sticky and unpleasant-smelling underneath or in the middle. (If the beans aren't dry enough, the excess moisture settles to the bottom and the beans spoil.) When pinched, the cake feels mushy or falls apart. Any other color besides white, black or gray tempeh should be thrown away.

Preserving Tempeh:

A small batch of tempeh will keep in the refrigerator for 3 or 4 days. Never stack packages of fresh tempeh together or heat will encourage culture growth. Steaming, boiling or freezing will kill the growth. It keeps well in the freezer. Cool, seal it in air–tight plastic bags and don't stack it until completely frozen. It will keep 6 months or more. Let frozen tempeh thaw out at room temperature, then steam and use.

Steaming Tempeh:

Steam tempeh for 10 minutes before using in cooked recipes unless recipe is baked. Simmer or steam for 15 minutes if you are using it in salad, sandwiches, or in spreads.

TEMPEH STARTER
Order Tempeh Starter from:

The Tempeh Lab
P.O. Box 208
Summertown, TN 38483

Other Methods for Splitting and Hulling Whole Soybeans

Method I: Boil whole dry soybeans 20 minutes. Turn off heat, cover, and let stand for two hours. Then split beans by squeezing them with a kneading motion, a handful at a time, till they're all split. Or, place a thin layer of beans inside a shallow tray; using a closed-mesh potato masher, in a rocking motion, split beans in half. (Some will break up smaller.)

Boil split beans one hour, skimming the hulls. Proceed with step number 2 on page 83.

Method II: Soak beans overnight or by method described above. Chop into large bits with blender or food grinder. Boil 25 minutes (save liquid for use in baking). Proceed with step number 2 on page 83. Place ¼" deep in tempeh container. Pack lightly.

RECIPES FOR SOYBEAN TEMPEH

INDONESIAN FRIED TEMPEH

Soak thin slices of **tempeh** in **brine** (4 tsp. salt in a quart of water) for 20 minutes. Pan fry in **oil** or **margarine** or deep fry till golden brown. Try it topped with sauce, baked on pizza, or in sandwiches.

PAN FRIED TEMPEH

In a skillet, fry squares of **tempeh** in **oil** or **margarine** on one side till golden brown. Add ¼-½ **cup lightly salted water** and cover immediately. When the water steams away, flip the squares. Fry and steam on the other side.

ALBERT'S TEMPEH TOPPING

Serves 6-8

½ **cup tomato paste**   ½ **cup sugar**
2 **tsp. hot curry powder**   ½ **tsp. salt**

Mix and let stand. Makes 1 cup, enough for one pound of tempeh.

BARBEQUED TEMPEH

Cover the bottom of a **margarined** baking dish with a thin layer of *Barbeque Sauce* (p.81), then cover with pieces of **deep fried tempeh** and then a thick layer of *Barbeque Sauce*. Bake at 350° until it bubbles.

Or, you can baste pieces of deep fried tempeh with the sauce as you grill them over a charcoal grill.

Fried tempeh

SWEET AND SOUR TEMPEH

Cut **tempeh** into strips ½" wide. Deep fry.
Sauce:

2 **carrots,** sliced
1 **onion,** sliced
2 **bell peppers,**
chopped
⅓ **cup oil**
½ **tsp. garlic powder**
½ **tsp. ginger**

½ **cup water**
½ **cup vinegar**
2 **Tbsp. soy sauce**
6 **Tbsp. sugar**
12-**oz. can pine-**
apple chunks
2 **tsp. cornstarch**
2 **tsp. water**

Saute carrots, onions and peppers in oil with garlic and ginger. Mix ½ cup water with vinegar, soysauce, sugar, and juice from canned pineapple. Pour sauce over vegetables and bring to a boil.

Mix cornstarch with 2 tsp. water. When sauce boils, add cornstarch mixture, let thicken, and add pineapple.

Serve tempeh on bed of rice. Pour sauce over it.

CREAMED TEMPEH

Serves 5-6

Place **4 cups tempeh strips** (½" wide and 2" long) in a frying pan. Add **1¼ cups water** and **1¼ tsp. salt,** cover and steam until the water is gone. Remove lid and add **4-5 Tbsp. oil.** Fry at medium heat until golden brown.

To prepare white sauce , melt **5 Tbsp. margarine.** Whisk in **5 Tbsp. white flour** to form a smooth paste, then whisk in **2½ cups soymilk, 1½ tsp. salt,** and a **dash of pepper.** Cook at a low boil for 3 minutes.

Combine tempeh and white sauce, and serve over toast or rice.

TEMPEH CACCIATORE

Serves 6

Steam 12-18 pieces of fresh **tempeh** in a skillet for 5 minutes. Cool. Mix together **½ cup flour, salt** and **pepper.** Dip each piece of tempeh in mixture and fry with **1 cup chopped onions** in **oil** till tempeh is golden brown on both sides. Add the sauce below and simmer 1 hour.

1 quart tomato sauce	**1 tsp. basil**
1 tsp. salt	**1 tsp. oregano**
1 bay leaf	**1/8 tsp. sweet**
2 cloves garlic, minced	**marjoram**
1/8 tsp. thyme	**1 Tbsp. sugar**

Serve with salad and garlic bread.

TEMPEH WITH PEPPERS

Steam **8 oz. tempeh** for 10 minutes. Cut in strips ¼″ thick. Mix together: **2 Tbsp. soy sauce, 1 cup vegetable stock, 1 tsp. garlic powder.** Toss tempeh with sauce and let stand while slicing **1 onion** and **1 pepper.** Drain the tempeh, saving the liquid. Heat a large skillet or wok and add **2 Tbsp. olive oil.** Quickly brown the tempeh, remove. Add **2 Tbsp. olive oil** to pan and cook the onions and peppers until softened. Dissolve **1 Tbsp. cornstarch** in marinade, pour over onions. Cook until thickened and stir in the browned tempeh.

SAUSAGE PATTIES

Steam **8 ounces of tempeh** for 15 minutes. Cool, grate on coarse side of grater. Mix for seasonings ½ **tsp. each sage, marjoram, thyme** and **cumin.** Add **2 Tbsp. unbleached white flour.** Then stir in: **2 Tbsp. warm water, 2 Tbsp. oil** and **2 Tbsp. soy sauce.** Press firmly into thin patties. Fry in a little **oil** until browned on both sides.

Italian Sausage: Grate the **steamed tempeh.** Mix for seasonings: **2 cloves garlic, pressed, ½ tsp. red pepper flakes, 1 tsp. oregano, ¼ tsp. black pepper, 2 Tbsp. flour.** Combine tempeh, seasonings, **2 Tbsp. oil** and **2 Tbsp. soy sauce.** Press into thin patties or crumble on top of pizza before it is baked.

SAUERBRATEN

Cut **8 ounce cake of tempeh** in half crosswise, so you have 2 thin slabs. Cut each into 1″ squares. Mix together for a marinade:

1 cup apple juice
1 cup water
1 bay leaf
6 peppercorns
2 Tbsp. catsup
2 Tbsp. vinegar
1 tsp. powdered ginger
6 whole cloves
1 Tbsp. Worchestershire sauce
2 cloves of garlic, cut in half

Pour over tempeh and let soak several hours. Then remove tempeh and save marinade for sauce. Fry the tempeh pieces in a hot pan with a little oil until they are browned, turning. Place in casserole.

Roast over low heat until you can smell it:
2 Tbsp. unbleached flour

Stir in **3 Tbsp. oil** and cook a few minutes. Then add the strained marinade and cook until it is bubbly. Pour the sauce over tempeh. Cover and bake at 350° about 30 minutes. Serve over rice or noodles.

MISO

Miso is a fermented food made from soybeans, grains and salt. It originated in Japan and is used as a base for soups and sauces. Miso is a thick paste and comes in several varieties ranging from light and slightly sweet to dark and robust. It's salty, like soy sauce, so a little flavors a lot.

Miso is high in protein and B vitamins and contains healthful micro–organisms that aid digestion. It will keep for months in a tightly closed container in your refrigerator.

Thin miso with warm water before adding to recipes. In soups, it should be added last and never boiled. It's delicious spread on crackers or on tofu in sandwiches, or used instead of salt on fried tofu.

MISO SALAD DRESSING

Put in a pint jar and stir to dissolve:
   2 cloves garlic, minced
   2 Tbsp. light miso
   1 inch fresh ginger, minced
   2 tsp. honey
   2 Tbsp. warm water
Add to jar:
   ⅓ cup vinegar
   ⅔ cup oil
Cover jar and shake well. Serve over lettuce or fresh spinach leaves.

CREAMY MISO SPREAD

Combine in a small bowl and set aside:
3 Tbsp. light miso
2 Tbsp. warm water
Blend until creamy:
½ cup tofu, crumbled
2 Tbsp. oil
2 Tbsp. lemon juice or vinegar
1 tsp. honey
Blend in the miso and water.

JAPANESE MISO SOUP

This is a traditional soup, served for breakfast in Japan.
Make 4 cups of vegetable stock by combining:
1 Tbsp. vegetable bouillon granules
4 cups hot water
Mix in a small bowl:
3 Tbsp. dark miso
1 tsp. honey
¼ cup warm stock
Stir until free of lumps.
Cut into small cubes and place in 6 soup bowls:
½ to 1 pound tofu
Bring the vegetable stock to a boil. Remove from heat and stir in the miso, mixing well. Add **1 Tbsp. soy sauce** and **¼ cup chopped green onions.**
Ladle the soup into bowls over the tofu.

This recipe provides your family with a highly nutritious and good-tasting beverage. An 8-ounce glass supplies about 9 grams of protein, slightly more than found in the same amount of cow's milk. Soymilk is low in calories and contains no cholesterol. A pound of soybeans will make a gallon of soymilk and can cost your family less than 15¢ if you buy your beans at a co-op or feed store. (If you buy your beans at a feed store, *be sure they aren't treated with mercury—mercury is poison.*)

Serve soymilk hot or chilled, flavored with various extracts, fruit, carob, or cocoa. It makes a smooth milkshake mixed in a blender with a little oil and flavoring.

Preparation:

Rinse 2½ **cups whole soybeans** and soak in **5 cups of water**, following one of the methods described below. After the beans are soaked, transfer to a colander and rinse again.

Soak Method I: Soak rinsed soybeans in a bowl or pot of **cold water** for 8-10 hours or overnight. In hot weather the soaking beans should be kept in the refrigerator to prevent souring. Slightly soured beans will make a thinner milk.

Soak Method II: For quick soaking, pour **boiling water** over rinsed beans and allow to soak 2-4 hours. Beans will double in size and be free of wrinkles when done. They will have a flat, not concave, surface when split in half.

Grinding the Beans:

Method I: Combine in a blender **1 cup soaked soybeans** and **2½ cups water**. You can use either cold water or nearly boiling water in this step. The advantage of using hot water is a slightly milder flavor and a shorter wait for your mixture to come to a boil. Blend the beans at high speed to a fine slurry (about 1 minute). Pour contents into a large heavy pot or double boiler (it won't burn as easily). Repeat blender process until all beans are blended.

Method II: Grind the soaked beans using a hand grain-mill or a food grinder (use the plate with the smallest holes). When using a hand grain-mill, set the grind pretty tight, so that it easily allows a fine but slightly gritty bean paste to pass through the stones. With finely ground beans, more protein will be

released into the milk and the yield of tofu will be higher. However, if the grind is too fine, it will be difficult to strain and will cause a pulpy soymilk. Add the **ground bean paste** to a pot of **13 cups boiling water**.

Cooking the Soymilk:

Cook the soymilk in a 1½-2 gallon heavy-bottom pot or double boiler. Set over a medium-high flame and bring to a boil, stirring occasionally. Watch the pot carefully. When the soymilk first starts to boil, turn down the heat immediately and simmer at a low boil for 20 minutes. It's important to be right there with your pot at this step. Soymilk will foam up and boil over quickly, so watch it carefully. If you use an electric stove, remove the pot from the burner when it comes to a boil while you adjust the heat.

Straining the Soymilk:

Set a cloth-lined colander (thin cotton or nylon) over a pot with at least 1-gallon capacity. After the soymilk is cooked, pour or ladle it into the colander, catching the pulp in the cloth and the milk in the pot below. Twist the cloth

tightly closed. With a wooden spoon or a jar, press on the bag to extract as much milk as possible. To rinse through any milk left in the pulp, re-open the cloth, stir in **2 cups boiling water**, twist and press again. Set pulp aside to be used in cooking (see p.145).

Cooling the Soymilk:

You can drink the soymilk hot or you can cool it by placing the pot in a sink of cold water, replenishing the cold water as necessary. When cooled, transfer into covered containers and refrigerate or freeze. The quicker the soymilk is cooled and the colder it is kept, the longer it will last. It has an approximate shelf life of 4-5 days. If it starts to sour, use it for baking in cakes, biscuits, or bread.

Unlike cow's milk, soymilk contains very few natural sugars. For drinking, most people prefer to add a sweetener, vanilla or cocoa, and a dash of salt. Soymilk can be made thicker or thinner by adjusting the proportion of beans to water in this recipe. Soymilk can be used to replace cow's milk in any recipe . . .

. . . except maybe one.

VANILLA MILKSHAKE

2 cups soymilk **2 Tbsp. oil**
2–3 ice cubes **1 tsp. pure vanilla**
¼ cup sugar **1/8 tsp. salt**

Combine in a blender until ice is well blended. Serve at once. For a thicker milkshake, blend in an extra cup of ice.

Milkshakes can also be made by whipping ice bean (see pp.104-106) and adding a touch of soymilk to thin it down.

SOY NOG

3 cups soymilk **¼-½ tsp. rum extract**
½ cup sugar **pinch nutmeg**
1 tsp. pure vanilla **1-2 Tbsp. oil**

Combine in blender until smooth and serve hot or cold.

BANANA SMOOTHIE

1 cup soymilk
1 cup ice
3 medium-size bananas
2 Tbsp. honey
dash of salt

Combine ingredients in a blender and blend until smooth. Serve immediately.

BANANA SMOOTHIE # 2

A good smoothie can be made with **frozen bananas** instead of ice. Peel and freeze bananas in a plastic container or plastic bag. Start blending **2 cups soymilk, 2 Tbsp. honey,** and **a dash of salt** in blender and add about **4 small frozen bananas.** Drop in one banana at a time. The soymilk will get thick and frothy and should be served immediately. More honey may be added if you want it sweeter.

VANILLA PUDDING

¾ cup sugar   3 cups soymilk
¼ cup cornstarch ¼ cup margarine
¼ tsp. salt   2 tsp. vanilla

Combine sugar, cornstarch and salt in a medium saucepan. Gradually blend in the milk, stirring until smooth. Cover and cook over a low heat, boiling gently for about 5 minutes. Remove from heat, blend in margarine and vanilla. Pour into dessert cups or a baked pie crust and chill. Top with *Tofu Whipped Topping.*

CHOCOLATE PUDDING

Mix together well:

⅓ cup cocoa   ¼ cup cornstarch
¾ cup sugar   (⅓ cup cornstarch
¼ tsp. salt   if making a pie)

Then add **3 cups soymilk,** whipping constantly. Bring this mixture to a boil over medium heat, still whipping constantly, then lower the heat and cover. Let boil gently for 5-10 minutes.

Remove from heat and whip in:

3 Tbsp. margarine
1½ tsp. vanilla

Pour into a bowl or baked pie crust, chill, and serve with *Tofu Whipped Topping.*

LEMON PIE FILLING

Combine in saucepan:
1½ cups sugar
½ cup + 1 Tbsp. cornstarch
¼ tsp. salt
Whisk in **2¼ cups water** (or half water
and half soymilk) and bring to a boil over
medium heat. Cook 3-5 minutes, stirring
often with a whisk. Remove from heat.
Stir in **3 Tbsp. margarine** and slowly add
¾ cup lemon juice and grated rind of 2 lemons.
Pour into *Graham Cracker Crust*(p.135). Chill.
Before serving spread with *Tofu Whipped Topping.*

TOFU WHIPPED TOPPING

1 cup soft tofu
¼ cup oil
2 Tbsp. honey or **sugar**
1 Tbsp. lemon juice
1 tsp. vanilla
dash of salt
Blend until smooth and creamy, scraping sides
of blender inward. Whip a little just before serving if needed.

Chocolate and Vanilla Pudding with Bananas

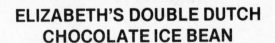

ELIZABETH'S DOUBLE DUTCH CHOCOLATE ICE BEAN

1¾ cups sugar
½ cup cocoa
real good pinch salt
½ tsp. vanilla
¼ cup oil
3 cups soymilk

Put sugar in blender, cocoa on top, and salt and vanilla. Put in half the milk and blend till the cocoa is smooth. Then add the rest of the milk and oil and blend till mixed.

Follow directions for freezing from your hand-crank machine or electric ice cream machine.

VANILLA ICE BEAN

1 cup sugar
3 cups soymilk
1½-2 tsp. pure vanilla
¼ cup oil (more or less, depending on how rich you want it)
a pinch of salt

Blend this in a blender, then add **¾ tsp. liquid lecithin.** Blend it—be sure to blend it well. Put it in your machine and let 'er crank.

PINEAPPLE SHERBET

1 cup crushed pineapple
2 cups soymilk
2 Tbsp. oil
1/8 cup sugar
¼ tsp. vanilla
dash salt

Blend the fruit with half the soymilk and oil and the rest of the ingredients. When it's smooth, add the rest of the milk and the rest of the oil.

Follow directions for freezing from your hand-crank or electric ice cream machine.

HONEY BANANA ICE BEAN

Blend:

3 cups soymilk	4-6 Tbsp. oil
1 large or 2 medium bananas	½ cup honey
	dash of salt

Freeze mix in an ice cream machine.

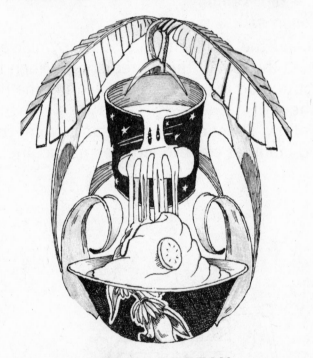

CAROB ICE BEAN

3 cups soymilk	¼ cup oil
1 cup sugar	1 tsp. vanilla
¾ cup carob	dash of salt

Blend 1 cup soymilk, sugar, carob and oil into a smooth paste. Blend in remaining ingredients. Freeze in an ice cream machine.

STRAWBERRY FROGURT

3 cups soy yogurt
1½ cups strawberries
1¼ cups sugar (use ¼ cup less with
 frozen, sweetened strawberries)
dash of salt
¼ cup oil

Blend together and freeze in an ice cream machine.

Ice Bean

ORANGE VANILLA FROGURT

3 cups soy yogurt
1 cup sugar
3 Tbsp. frozen orange juice concentrate
1-2 tsp. vanilla
dash of salt
¼ cup oil

Combine in a blender and freeze in an ice cream machine.

Yogurt can be made from soymilk as well as cow's milk. To make yogurt, place inverted, clean jars in a pot of water. Bring water to a boil and let it boil for at least 2 minutes. Throw in the caps and a clean rubber spatula to be used to stir in the starter later.

Heat the **soymilk** to a boil and hold for 30 seconds, stirring *constantly.* Pour into hot sterile jars. Cover. Let cool to about 110°, or until the jar feels hot to your wrist but does not burn.

Add **2 Tbsp. yogurt** to each quart. (This can be from a good brand of plain cow's milk yogurt to start with, if a commercial yogurt starter isn't available.) Stir briskly with the sterilized spatula, cover and incubate for 2-6 hours at approximately 105°. Yogurt is done if, when you tilt the jar gently, it separates easily and cleanly from the jar sides. Refrigerate. Good plain, salted, or with sweetener and cut up fruit such as bananas or peaches.

For a thicker yogurt, make a thicker soymilk by adding either less water or more beans to the soymilk recipe. A jar of this yogurt can be set aside and used to start an additional batch of yogurt. Use 3-4 Tbsp. of this yogurt per 1 qt. of soymilk.

Yogurt can also be made in a pressure cooker because of its tight-sealing lid. Bring milk to a boil for 30 seconds. Put the lid and jiggler on the pot and set in a sink of cold water to cool. Check it in about 10-15 minutes. Shake the pot a few times to evenly distribute the heat of the soy-milk, and remove lid. The soymilk should be fairly hot (about 110°). You can use a sterile candy thermometer. Stir in starter with a sterilized spoon, replace lid and jiggler, and incubate as suggested below.

Incubation:

Put jars or pressure cooker in a warm place such as a gas oven with a pilot light, or a closed insulated picnic cooler box with a drop light turned on inside. Or, put the jars in the oven, turn the oven on to 150° for 3 minutes, then turn it off and let the yogurt incubate, undisturbed, for 2-6 hours.

Yogurt with Peach Slices

For making transfers and larger batches of yogurt:
    Yogurt starter is available in some health food stores as a dry powder. A good "mother" culture can be made by culturing one quart of soy milk with the starter. From this quart jar you can inoculate 16 gallons of soymilk. About 1 Tbsp. of "mother" culture will make a quart and ¼ cup will make a gallon. Use the original quart jar to make another quart that will be your second generation. Remember to be very clean in order to keep your yogurt from getting contaminated. Keep your hands well washed. Should your yogurt get pink, fizzy or slimy, throw everything out, sterilize all equipment, and start again.

RICHARD'S YOGURT CHEESE

A delicious cheese can be made from **yogurt** by placing the fresh thick curds in a nylon or lightweight cotton cloth. Twist the cloth into a ball and tie with some thin cord. Hang this over a sink or a pot for a few hours. This will make a nice moist cheese. If you want a denser cheese, hang longer or press for a while. This cheese is a basis for cottage cheese, cream cheese, dips, salad dressings, and cheesecakes.

If your yogurt isn't nice and thick so that it will hang into curds easily, you can try heat-ing it some. The heat will help it to curd more and the curds will  be firmer and press out easier. The disadvantage with this is that the active yogurt cultures are killed by the heat and the cheese is drier. It makes a nice cheese, though!

YOGURT "COTTAGE CHEESE"

To make "cottage cheese," just sprinkle **salt** over a bowl of moist **yogurt cheese curds.** Serve on a lettuce leaf and garnish with paprika and a sprig of parsley.

YOGURT CREAM CHEESE

1 cup moist yogurt cheese
2 Tbsp. oil
1/8 tsp. salt
½ tsp. sugar

Blend ingredients in a blender until smooth. Pour into a dish and chill for an hour or two.

YOGURT WHIZ

This drink is best made with fresh fruit in season and is a great icy drink for a hot summer day.

1 cup yogurt
1 cup ice
1 cup fresh fruit (strawberries or raspberries are good)
2 Tbsp. sugar (more may be added depending on type of fruit used)
dash of salt

Combine ingredients in a blender and serve immediately.

YOGURT CHEESE CAKE

3 cups moist yogurt cheese
½ cup oil
½ cup honey or 1 cup sugar
1 tsp. vanilla
¼ tsp. salt

Combine ingredients in blender or food processor. When smooth, pour into partially baked cheesecake crust. Bake at 300° for about 1 hour or until center feels firm to a touch. Long slow baking is best for cheesecakes.

Crust for Cheesecake:
2 cups unbleached flour
⅓ cup sugar
¼ cup margarine
2 Tbsp. oil
2 Tbsp. water
dash cinnamon

Mix flour, sugar and cinnamon. Work in margarine and oil with fingers. Work in water. Pat on bottom and up sides of pie pan. Partially bake crust for 10 minutes at 350°. Then fill with cheesecake mixture and bake.

You'll notice when making or heating soymilk that a layer of skin will form on the top of the milk. This is caused by the oil in the milk rising to the top, and is called *yuba.* Yuba is considered a delicacy in Japan and China where they have small factories dedicated to making it.

The process is simple. Heat soymilk in a pot or shallow pan. When a good layer of yuba forms on the top, cut it around the edges to free it from the pot and slip a chopstick underneath the middle of it through to the other side. Lift up gently.

More than one layer of yuba will form on a pot of milk, so you can get a few sheets by keeping the milk hot and lifting off each layer of yuba as it forms.

Yuba can be scrambled while it's soft and fresh or can be hung to dry until it turns brittle. Dried yuba can be broken up and added to a dish of stir-fried vegetables. (Dried yuba can be stored in the refrigerator.)

Lifting Yuba off the Soymilk

A layer of film will also form on the bottom and sides of the pot when making soymilk. This is also a form of yuba and can be scraped off the pot with a knife or metal spatula. This yuba is usually a tougher consistency and can sometimes be filled with tofu and vegetables, rolled, tucking the ends in, and fried until crispy (like a blintze!).

FRIED YUBA

Place ½ **cup soft yuba** (cut in strips) in a hot frying pan with **1-2 Tbsp. margarine.** Sprinkle with **salt** and **pepper** and **nutritional yeast flakes** ☆ (opt.). Fry till slightly golden, turning once.

☆ See page 58.

Tofu has been a staple food for millions of people in Asia for centuries. Tofu contains high quality protein, no cholesterol, is low in calories, and is inexpensive to purchase or make at home.

Tofu will keep for a week or two in the refrigerator. Keep covered with cold water and change the water daily, If tofu begins to have a slightly sour smell, use it right away in a baked recipe. If tofu is purchased in a vacuum package, watch expiration date.

Tofu can be frozen right in the vacuum package or tightly wrapped in plastic or foil. Frozen tofu will be light tan in color and chewy in consistency. Defrost and squeeze out the excess liquid before using in a recipe. It's good cooked with barbeque sauce or gravy, use in pot pie or curry.

There are different types and textures of tofu, and this is good to know when cooking with it or making it. Some tofu contains more water and is softer and silkier. This is the best kind to use for blender products or soft spreads. Other tofu is denser and firmer and is better for slicing, deep frying or crumbling, but doesn't blend as smoothly. Techniques for making both kinds of tofu at home are given in the following recipes.

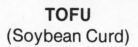

TOFU
(Soybean Curd)

To make tofu, follow the recipe for making soymilk on page 95, changing the proportions to **3 cups water** for every **1 cup soaked soybeans.** After the soymilk is strained and while it's still very hot, prepare the solidifier. Combine **1 cup warm water** with:

- **1½-2 tsp. nigari,** or
- **1½-2 tsp. epsom salts,** or
- **¼ cup vinegar,** or
- **¼ cup lemon juice.**

Nigari is our preferred solidifier. It is made by removing the sodium and water from sea water. The remaining minerals are the nigari in a crystallized form. Nigari produces a nice firm tofu, more subtle in flavor than tofu made with epsom salts or vinegar, and yields a good amount of protein. It also supplies your body with added minerals, among them potassium, magnesium, and calcium.

Epsom salts (magnesium sulfate) is good for a high yield of tofu and is easy to find in a drug store.

Vinegar or lemon juice usually produces soft curds. However, if boiled for a few minutes they can become quite firm. Vinegar and lemon juice are easy to purchase and add a nice tart flavor to the tofu.

There are different variables to consider that affect the amount of solidifier to add when making tofu. The variety of beans used, the temperature of the soymilk (should be about 185°), the strength of the solidifier, and the method of curding, all affect the final product. After making tofu a few times you'll develop a feel for how much to add and when.

Curding the Soymilk:

While the strained soymilk is fresh and hot, stir slowly with a wooden spoon in a circular motion and pour in half of the solidifying solution. Slowly stir in the opposite direction to create a current that will mix the solidifier in well. Sprinkle a small amount more solidifier (¼ cup) over the top of the soymilk. Cover the pot to retain the heat for proper curding, and allow the milk to set undisturbed for 5 minutes. The tofu will start to form large white curds. If the soymilk is still milky-looking, poke the top few inches gently to activate curding and then gently stir in the rest of the solidifying solution if necessary. Cover pot again and let set a couple more minutes.

The end result here should be large white curds floating in a clear yellow liquid called *whey.* If there is any milky liquid left, stir it gently into the whey to help it curd. If after a minute of stirring there isn't any noticeable difference in curd and whey formation, make up some additional solidifying solution using approximately ½ tsp. nigari or epsom salts, or 1 Tbsp. vinegar dissolved in ¼ cup hot water. Stir it gently into the pot. Always stir gently to prevent breaking up the curds, and only stir the top few inches of the pot. Take pokes to the bottom of the pot in various places to allow any milk trapped between the curds to come up to the top where it will be curded by the whey. When all of the soymilk is formed into curds and there is only clear yellow whey left, the tofu is ready for the pressing box.

If there is a lot of whey and only a few curds it's possible that the solidifier was too strong or was added too fast, or the beans may not have been ground fine enough, resulting in a thin milk and low yield.

Curding Soymilk

Pressing the Tofu:

Set up a tofu press or a colander in the sink and line with nylon tricot or curtain mesh. Set the pot next to it. Using a ladle or measuring cup, and a large tea strainer or colander with small holes, prepare to ladle the curds into the cloth. To do this, set the strainer in the pot and let it fill with whey. Ladle out whey until most of it is out of the pot. This will help the curds form together for a nice solid tofu. After the whey is removed, ladle the curds into the press, cover with the cloth and put on the lid. If using a colander, place a small plate on top of the tofu.

To press the tofu, use a heavy weight that will fit nicely inside the press. A jar of water or a clean heavy rock or brick can be used. Press for 20-30 minutes. For firmer tofu, use a heavier weight or press longer.

Remove the weight and lid. Tofu should be firm to the touch. Fold back the cloth and re-set the lid directly on top of the tofu. Turn the tofu upside down so the tofu is sitting on the lid. Remove press or colander and gently peel off the cloth. The tofu can be set in a sink or bowl of cold water to get cool and firm.

Tofu should be stored in a container of cold water in the refrigerator. Change the water daily to help preserve freshness. If stored properly, it will keep up to a week.

(Clockwise): Tofu in cloth, Soybeans, Soymilk, and a block of Tofu.

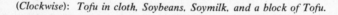

Here are a couple of frequently asked questions:

Q. I followed the instructions but my tofu is still milky among the curds. I added a little more solidifier but still nothing. What should I do now?

A. Probably what happened was the soymilk didn't maintain enough heat during the curding process or sat too long between curdings. Set your pot of curds back on the stove and re-heat. As it heats up it will develop into curds and whey. If it still doesn't, add more solidifier.

Q. During my first curding, the soymilk instantly separated into curds and a lot of whey. Is this common?

A. What happened here was that too much solidifier was added during the first curding. This could have been caused by the milk being too thin (maybe the grind wasn't fine enough), in which case the amount of solidifier added was proportionately too strong. It's also possible that the solidifier was too strong. If you're using vinegar, check it out—it comes in different strengths and might need to be diluted.

Here are some good tips for tofu makers:

- The hotter the soymilk is when curded, the firmer the curds will be. If a very firm tofu is desired, the curds may be placed back on the heat and boiled a few minutes.
- For the highest yield of tofu, the curding should be done slowly (in a few stages). This produces large, soft curds and yields a tofu high in water content. This tofu is especially good for blender products and *Soft Scrambled Tofu.*
- Gently stir the top few inches of the soymilk when you're checking the curds and take a few pokes to the bottom of the pot. This helps to activate the curding and can sometimes be done in place of adding more solidifier. The poking also helps to bring up any milk that's trapped between curds at the bottom of the pot.
- Too much solidifier will give the tofu a strong flavor that isn't as appetizing. Tofu should have a subtle flavor.

Whey

Whey is the clear yellow liquid left over when making tofu. Except when epsom salt has been used as a solidifier, the whey can be used in bread or soup stocks. It also makes a good hair rinse.

Whey acts as a natural detergent and will suds easily if stirred. It is good for washing and soaking the pots and cloths used during the tofu-making process.

Care and Maintenance of Press and Cloth

Clean your milk-making equipment and cloth well after each use. A mild soap solution may be used. Cloths can be soaked in bleach water occasionally. Whey can be used to wash your equipment, also. A vegetable brush is a good cleaning tool for your colander, press and cloth.

The pot used for cooking the soymilk is the most difficult piece to clean. A copper or stainless steel scrubber can be used. Also, a metal spatula comes in handy for the preliminary scraping of the film that forms along the sides and bottom of the pot. For easiest cleaning, soak the pot in cold water immediately after using. Keep everything clean as you make your soymilk. The quicker your utensils are washed or rinsed, the easier they are to clean.

DEEP FRIED TOFU

Slice **tofu** ½ to ¾" thick. (Or cut into cubes to use in spaghetti sauce). Dry on paper towels. **Peanut** or **corn oil** are best for deep frying. Fry tofu until brown and crispy, drain on paper towels and sprinkle with **nutritional yeast flakes** (see p.58), or **salt** and **pepper.** Good served with tarter sauce or in sandwiches with salad dressing. Deep Fried Tofu can be basted with barbeque sauce and cooked on a grill or cover slices with barbeque sauce, bake at 350° for 10 minutes, turn and baste, cook 10 minutes more. Good in buns.

Pan Fried Tofu

PAN FRIED TOFU

Slice **tofu** ¼ to ½" thick. Dip in **flour, a breading or in soy sauce.** Pan fry in a little hot **oil** until golden brown.

Breading:
Mix together:
½ cup flour
2 Tbsp. nutritional yeast flakes ☆(opt.)
½ tsp. salt
½ tsp. each basil and **oregano**
dash of garlic powder, pepper
Dip moist slices of tofu into breading, then quickly pan fry in a well oiled skillet.

Cornmeal Breading:
½ cup cornmeal
½ tsp. salt
½ tsp. paprika
dash pepper, garlic powder

BARBEQUE TOFU

Pan fry or deep fry ½-¾" slices of **tofu** (see p.124). Line the bottom of a baking pan with the fried tofu and cover with *Barbeque Sauce* (p.83). Bake at 350° for about 20 minutes. Serve with rice or in a sandwich.

If you are using *Deep Fried Tofu*, you can grill it over charcoals in a barbeque pit while basting with the barbeque sauce.

☆ See page 58.

TOFU POT PIE

Combine in a small bowl:
  ¼ cup flour
  1 Tbsp. nutritional yeast flakes ☆
  1 tsp. salt
  ½ tsp. garlic powder
Add and stir to coat:
  2 cups tofu, cut in ½″ cubes
Heat a skillet and saute tofu in:
  2 Tbsp. oil
until lightly browned. Add to the pan:
  1 cup onions, cut in wedges
  ½ cup celery, sliced
When onions are soft, add other vegetables, such as **cooked carrots, whole kernel corn, fresh** or **frozen peas** or **green beans.** Make *Golden Gravy* (p.63) and add the vegetables. Place pie filling in a casserole and top with your choice of a **pastry crust** (p.132) or **biscuit dough, mashed potatoes** or **crushed cornflakes.** Bake at 375° for 30 to 40 minutes until top is lightly browned.

☆ See page 58.

TOFU "GRILLED CHEESE" SANDWICHES
Makes 10

Stir **2½ cups** lightly salted, crumbled **tofu** into 1 recipe of *Melty Nutritional Yeast "Cheese"* (p.59). Spread between two slices of **bread. Margarine** the outsides and grill. **Tomato** and **onion** slices may be added also before grilling.

This is one of our kids' favorites.

SOFT SCRAMBLED TOFU

Saute some **onions** and add crumbled or mashed **tofu** along with **salt, pepper, nutritional yeast flakes** ☆ (opt.), and **soy sauce** to taste. A little **turmeric** can be added for color. Fry the tofu until browned.

☆ See page 58.

TOFU SPINACH PIE

Saute until onions are soft:

1 cup onions

¼ cup oil

Stir in:

2 cups spinach, chopped and cooked

Remove from heat. Mix in:

2 cups tofu, crumbled

1 tsp. garlic powder

2 Tbsp. nutritional yeast flakes ☆

½ tsp. salt

1 Tbsp. lemon juice

Place in a partially baked pie shell, cover top with an unbaked crust. Slash top crust in several places. Bake pie at 375° for 25 to 30 minutes until golden brown.

Pie Crust: *Makes two 9" shells*

Mix together in a bowl:

2 cups flour

1 tsp. salt

Work **½ cup margarine** into this with your fingers. Add a **scant ½ cup cold water**, stirring as little as possible to form a ball.

Divide into 2 balls and roll out to 1/8" thickness. Prick the pie shell in the pan with a fork a number of times before baking to prevent bubbles. For a partially baked shell, bake at 400° for approximately 10-15 minutes (till lightly browned on edges).

☆ See page 58.

TOFU NOODLES

Mix well in a large bowl:

4 cups crumbled tofu
6 cups flour
1 Tbsp. salt

Add about **1 cup water** (this will vary depending on how wet your tofu is). It should make a moist dough that will stay together when kneaded. Knead it in the bowl until it holds together enough in a ball to be kneaded on a board. Knead 4-5 minutes on the board to develop the gluten in the flour. The dough should spring back when you poke your finger into it.

Divide the dough into 4 parts. Roll out one part at a time on a floured board to 1/10" thick. Sprinkle flour generously over the dough and fold it over gently into a long roll. Cut noodles ¼" wide using a sharp knife. Fluff the noodles with your fingers to unroll them.

Put into **boiling salted water,** bring back to a boil and boil 3-4 minutes. Drain and run cold water over the noodles to wash out excess starch. Add **margarine, salt** and **pepper** to taste.

This is a good high-protein dish for kids.

TOFU MANICOTTI
(Stuffed Noodles)

Prepare *Manicotti Noodles* (p.131) or use ½ lb. large manicotti noodles.

Filling:

Saute **1 cup chopped onions** in **3-4 Tbsp. margarine** or **oil**. Add:

   1½ cups chopped cooked spinach
   2½ cups mashed tofu
   salt and **garlic** to taste

Stuff the noodles and place them side by side in a greased baking pan that has a small amount of water in the bottom. Cover with *Tomato Sauce* below:

Tomato Sauce:

2 cups tomato sauce	**1/8 tsp. marjoram**
1 cup water	**1 tsp. salt**
1 tsp. garlic powder	**1 Tbsp. oil**
½ tsp. oregano	**2 tsp. sugar**
1 tsp. basil	

Simmer 20 minutes and pour over the stuffed noodles. Next pour a thin layer of *Melty Nutritional Yeast "Cheese"* (opt.) (p.59) over the top, cover with aluminum foil, and bake at 350° for 20 minutes if using home-made noodles, or 40-45 minutes if using un-cooked, packaged manicotti noodles.

CREPE NOODLES FOR MANICOTTI
Makes approximately 10

2 cups white flour
2¼ cups water
½ tsp. salt, scant

Mix flour, water and salt together into a thin, smooth batter. Use more water if necessary. Pour about ⅓ cup of batter into hot, lightly greased skillet and immediately swirl skillet so the batter spreads out evenly and thinly, like a crepe. When the edge of the noodle curls up a little, flip it over and let it cook for about 10 seconds, then remove. The noodles can be stacked. Fill each crepe with a row of filling, roll, and place in pan, folded side down.

Tofu Manicotti

TOFU ONION QUICHE

Fry until the onion is limp:
1 large onion, sliced
2 Tbsp. margarine
Remove from pan. Add to pan:
1 Tbsp. margarine
2 cups mushrooms, sliced
Cook a few minutes. Combine in a processor or blender until creamy:
2 cups tofu
2 Tbsp. oil
½ tsp. garlic powder
2 Tbsp. lemon juice
1 tsp. salt or **1 Tbsp. soy sauce**
2 Tbsp. nutritional yeast flakes ☆ (opt.)
2 Tbsp. flour
Combine flour mixture, mushrooms and onions. Put in the bottom of an 9″ unbaked pie shell. Bake at 350° for 45 to 50 minutes, until filling is set in the middle.

Pie Shell: Mix **1 cup flour, ½ tsp. salt** and **⅓ cup oil.** Add just enough **warm water** to form a ball (about 2 Tbsp.). Roll out between two sheets of waxed paper and place in pie pan.

Broccoli Quiche: Instead of mushrooms and onions, use **broccoli flowerettes.** Steam them 5 minutes, drain, add to tofu mixture.

☆See page 58.

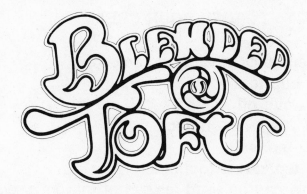

BLENDED TOFU
For making cheesecakes, cream pies,
dips, dressings, etc.

When you're blending with tofu it's good to know that all tofu isn't made the same. Different tofu makers incorporate different amounts of water into their product, so that some tofu is softer and silkier and some is slightly denser. This may affect the amount of liquid needed when blending tofu. For this reason, the liquid should be added last or as needed for good blending. A rubber scraper should be used to aid in blending the tofu. Scrape up and down the sides of the blender and fold tofu into the center. Blending small amounts at a time is also useful sometimes, especially when using firm tofu.

The oil content can be adjusted when blending tofu according to how rich a product you want. For dieters, blended tofu is tasty and creamy without any oil at all.

TOFU SOUR CREAM

Blend until creamy and smooth:
1 cup tofu
¼ cup oil
2 Tbsp. lemon juice
½ tsp. salt
1 tsp. sugar (optional)
This can be used instead of mayonnaise in sandwiches and burgers, or is a good base for dips. Delicious on top of baked potatoes with chives.

TARTAR SAUCE

1 cup tofu
3 Tbsp. oil
3 Tbsp. vinegar
½ tsp. salt
¼ cup onion, minced
1 tsp. wet mustard
Combine in blender and blend until smooth, using a rubber scraper on sides of the blender. Pour into a small dish and stir in **¼ cup sweet pickle relish.** Serve on fried tofu or tempeh, or use with soyburgers and other sandwiches. Instead of relish, you can use chopped parsley or stuffed olives.

TOFU CHEESECAKE

3 cups tofu
¼ cup lemon juice
½ cup oil
1 cup sugar
1 tsp. vanilla
a pinch of salt

Combine ingredients in a blender or processor until creamy, adding a little **water** at the end if needed to make tofu smooth. Pour into crust and bake at 325° for 50 minutes until set in the middle. Cool and top with fresh strawberries, drained crushed pineapple, sliced kiwi, sweet cherries or blueberries.

Graham Cracker Crust:
1½ cups graham crackers, crushed
¼ cup melted margarine or oil
1 Tbsp. sugar (opt.)

Mix crumbs, sugar and oil and press into the bottom and sides of a 9″ pie plate. This crust can be baked, cooled and filled with a pudding recipe. Bake for 10 to 12 minutes at 325°. You need not prebake it for cheesecake.

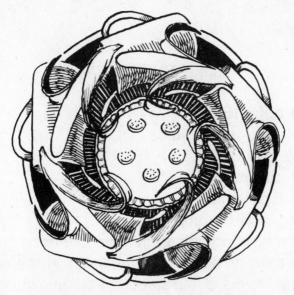

BANANA TOFU CREAM PIE
Makes one 9" pie

Blend in order given:
  2-3 ripe bananas
  2 tsp. pure vanilla
  1 Tbsp. lemon juice
  ½ cup oil
  1 cup sugar
  ¼ tsp. salt
Add:
  2½ cups firm tofu

Blend all ingredients until creamy and smooth. Use a rubber scraper to help blend in the tofu.

Pour the thick creamy blend into a prebaked pie shell and chill for 2-3 hours. Before serving, slice another banana in rounds and decorate the top of the pie.

CHOCOLATE TOFU CREAM PIE
This is a rich one

3 cups tofu
1 cup melted margarine
1½ cups sugar
¾ cup cocoa
2 tsp. vanilla
¼ tsp. salt
½ cup liquid, as needed for blending

Blend ingredients using the liquid to help blend the tofu. Try to blend as thick a cream as possible so it will set nicely when refrigerated. Pour into a **pre-baked pie shell,** top with *Tofu Whipped Topping* (p.95), and refrigerate a couple of hours.

It's convenient to keep frozen tofu on hand. It is easy to defrost at room temperature, in a microwave or by pouring hot water over the package. It soaks up marinades and has a chewy texture. It's good with vegetables in a won-ton wrapper for an "egg" roll filling, used in Chinese fried rice or a pot pie, crumbled onto pizza before baking, put in a pot of chili or in a curry sauce. Add it to *Golden Gravy* (p.63) and serve on rice or mashed potatoes, or enjoy it barbequed. Frozen tofu can be sliced, torn up or grated on the coarse side of a grater.

BARBEQUED FROZEN TOFU

Defrost a pound of frozen tofu and press out excess water. Cut it into thin slices or into finger size "ribs" and marinate in *Barbeque Sauce* (p.79). Place on a shallow oiled pan and bake at 375° for 10 minutes. Turn, baste with sauce and cook 10 minutes more.

Variation: To 1 cup of barbeque sauce, add **2 tsp. peanut butter, 2 tsp. honey** and a dash of **hot sauce.** Stir together, then spread on tofu. Bake as above or take to a "cook out" and grill. Baste with sauce when you turn the tofu.

SHISH KEBABS

Kebabs can also be made out of steamed tempeh cubes or chunk-style TVP soaked in hot water to reconstitute. Marinate for several hours if possible.

Mix in a bowl for a marinade:
¼ cup soy sauce
1 inch raw ginger,minced
½ cup water
2 Tbsp. oil
1 Tbsp. honey
2 Tbsp. lemon juice
1 tsp. peanut butter or **tahini**
¼ tsp. cayenne pepper
1 clove garlic, sliced

Press water out of **one pound of defrosted tofu.** Cut into 1″ cubes. Toss cubes in marinade, cover and let soak, stirring occasionally.

Prepare your choice of vegetables for kebabs:
green pepper, cut in squares
onions, cut in wedges
small, whole button mushrooms
cherry tomatoes
wedges of zucchini

Thread marinated cubes onto wooden or metal skewers, alternating tofu with vegetables. Place in pan, spoon marinade over. Cook under a hot broiler or on a grill, basting with marinade when you turn them over. Cook until vegetables are browned on edges. If kids don't like onions or peppers, use chunks of pineapple.

SLOPPY STEVE'S in BUNS

Defrost **1 pound of tofu,** squeeze out excess liquid, tear into small pieces.

Stir into tofu:
   2 Tbsp. soy sauce
   2 Tbsp. nutritional yeast flakes ☆ (p.58)

Fry together:
   2 Tbsp. oil
   ½ cup onions, chopped
   ½ cup celery, chopped or **1 green pepper,** chopped

When onions are soft, add the tofu to the pan and cook until it is browned and crunchy. Add a little more oil if needed. Add the sauce.

SAUCE:
   1 cup catsup
   2 tsp. vinegar
   2 tsp. lemon juice
   2 tsp. wet mustard
   2 Tbsp. brown sugar
   2 dashes hot sauce

Bring these to a boil and simmer a few minutes before adding the tofu. Cook about five minutes. Serve mixture in sandwich buns.

☆ See page 58.

Soy flour is ground up soybeans. Full fat soy flour contains all of the oil from the soybeans. It should be kept refrigerated to avoid the oil becoming rancid. Whole soybeans keep well, but once the hull of the bean is broken the oil will begin to oxidize. The texture of full fat soy flour is a cross between whole wheat flour and cornmeal.

Health food stores and co–ops carry soy flour, both full fat and low fat. Low fat soy flour has had most of its oil removed and will keep longer without refrigeration. Adding soy flour to bread, cookies and other baked goods will substantially increase the protein. It also helps retain moisture in baked goods.

SOY MILK
Using Soy Flour

Bring **12 cups water** to a boil. Dip some of the water out to make a paste with **4 cups soy flour.** Pour remaining water into paste, whisking out any lumps. Reduce heat to low and simmer 20 minutes, stirring occasionally. Use a kettle so it can't boil over. Strain the milk through a clean cloth and cool at once.

TOFU
From Soy Flour

This is a soft, creamy tofu good for blended tofu recipes, dips, puddings and pies. Use **one part full fat soy flour** to **3 parts boiling water.** Use a whisk to remove lumps, bring to a low boil and cook for 20 minutes. Strain and curd as described in the tofu instructions on page 116.

FARMER'S TOFU
From Soy Flour

This is a firm tofu, good for slicing and frying. It is made by soaking soy flour in water, straining it and then cooking and curdling the milk. Measure **4 cups full fat soy flour** into a large pan and whisk in **14 cups cold water.** Add only enough water at first to make a smooth paste, then whisk in remaining water. Soak for at least 30 minutes.

Take a pot of a least 2 gallon capacity and grease the sides and bottom well with oil. This will make cleaning easier after the cooking process. Set a colander over the pot and line it with a nylon or lightweight cotton cloth. Put the soaked mixture through the cloth and strain into the pot beneath (see straining soymilk, p.98). Now place the cloth with the flour in it into a bowl and add **2⅓ cups water.** Knead cloth again under water to remove any additional milk from the flour. Squeeze thoroughly and add this milky liquid to the pot.

Bring milk to a boil, lower heat. Prepare a solution of **¼ cup vinegar** or **2–3 tsp. nigari** in **1 cup hot water.** Stir the milk and pour in half the solution. If milk hasn't formed curds after a few minutes, stir in more of the solution. Simmer for 20 minutes. Follow the tofu instructions (p.116) for curding and pressing. For a softer tofu, cook the milk for 20 minutes, then remove from heat and curd it.

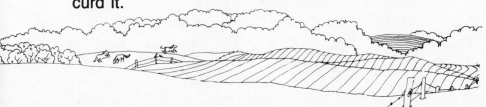

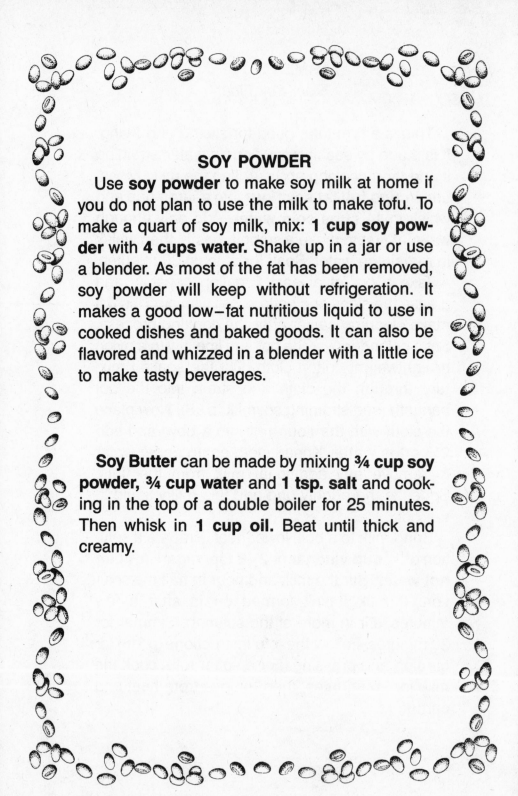

SOY POWDER

Use **soy powder** to make soy milk at home if you do not plan to use the milk to make tofu. To make a quart of soy milk, mix: **1 cup soy powder** with **4 cups water.** Shake up in a jar or use a blender. As most of the fat has been removed, soy powder will keep without refrigeration. It makes a good low–fat nutritious liquid to use in cooked dishes and baked goods. It can also be flavored and whizzed in a blender with a little ice to make tasty beverages.

Soy Butter can be made by mixing **¾ cup soy powder, ¾ cup water** and **1 tsp. salt** and cooking in the top of a double boiler for 25 minutes. Then whisk in **1 cup oil.** Beat until thick and creamy.

SOY "COFFEE"

Roast **soaked soybeans** in a medium (300°) oven on a cookie sheet, one bean deep. Remove from oven when beans are dark brown but not burned. Grind when hot, if possible. Store airtight. Percolate or simmer (don't boil or your coffee will be bitter) in a saucepan for about 5 minutes. Slightly less than 1 Tbsp. of soy coffee grounds per cup of water makes a tasty brew. It tastes a lot like coffee, but it's mellow on your nerves.

SOY "NUTS"

Soak **soybeans** overnight or put them in a pressure cooker with sufficient **water** and **1 Tbsp. oil.** Bring to full pressure and immediately remove from heat, allowing the beans to come down from pressure slowly. (Beans must be well soaked or partially cooked first, or they will be indigestible.) Drain well in a colander or strainer.

Method I: Heat **3 cups oil** to 400° and carefully add **1 cup soaked soybeans.** Fry on full flame for about 7 minutes or until golden brown. Remove beans and drain on paper towels. **Salt** to taste. Make sure the temperature of the oil is up to 400° at the start of each batch.

Method II: Place beans on an oiled cookie sheet, one bean deep, and bake in a moderate oven, turning occasionally, until golden brown, about 30-45 minutes.

Store soy nuts in an airtight container to keep crisp and serve as high-protein snacks.

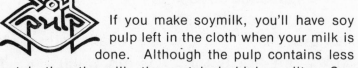 If you make soymilk, you'll have soy pulp left in the cloth when your milk is done. Although the pulp contains less protein than the milk, the protein is high quality. Soy pulp can be substituted for rice in many recipes. You can make *Soy Pulp Tempeh* out of it (see p.87), or it can be used in baked goods like cake and cookies, where it gives a coconutty flavor when combined with sugar and vanilla extract.

To be easily digested, soy pulp must be cooked until it's soft. Pressure cook the pulp for 20 minutes in ⅓ **cup water** for every **1 cup of pulp**; or steam it for 1½ hours.

SOYSAGE DOGS

Make *Soft Sandwich Bun* dough (p.171). Let dough rise for 5 minutes in a warm place. Roll out ¼" thick on a well-floured board and cut into 4" strips.

Starting at the side nearest you, place hot-dog shaped *Soysage* (p.147) on the dough. Roll it over once, cut, and pinch edges. Repeat with the rest of the dough. Put dogs almost touching on an oiled cookie sheet and let rise. Bake at 350° for about 20 minutes. Remove from oven and brush tops with **margarine.** Slit open, spread on mustard and stuff with sauerkraut.

SOYSAGE

4 cups soy pulp (from making soymilk,
    see p.93), or **cooked cracked soybeans**
2 cup whole wheat flour
1 cup wheat germ
¾ cup oil
1¼ cups soymilk (or other liquid)
1 cup nutritional yeast flakes ☆
1½ tsp. fennel seed
1 tsp. black pepper
¼ cup soy sauce
3 tsp. oregano
2 tsp. salt
½ tsp. cayenne
2 Tbsp. brown sugar
2 Tbsp. garlic powder
2 Tbsp. wet mustard
2 tsp. allspice

Mix ingredients. Oil an oven-proof bowl or empty tin can. Fill it and cover with tin foil. Steam on a rack for 1½ hours, or pressure cook in **5 cups water** for 30 minutes. Let it cool, then slice and fry.

☆ See page 58.

FRENCH CUCUMBER SALAD

Slice thinly into a bowl:
2 cucumbers, scored ☆
1 medium onion
Mix together:
½ cup cider vinegar
½ cup water
1 Tbsp. sugar
½ tsp. salt
¼ tsp. pepper
1 bay leaf
Let stand for one hour, refrigerated.

☆ To score cucumber, run a fork down the sides, making grooves that absorb the dressing. If cucumbers are not fresh, peel them before serving.

CUCUMBER DILL SALAD

Slice into a bowl:
2 cucumbers
Sprinkle with:
1 tsp. salt
Cover and chill for 30 minutes or longer. Drain, pressing out liquid. Add:
1 Tbsp. onion, chopped
1 Tbsp. vinegar
1 cup Tofu Sour Cream (p.134)
2 tsp. dill weed
Stir gently. Sprinkle top with dill. Keep chilled.

SPINACH SALAD

Wash and dry in a towel **1 pound** of **young spinach leaves.** Cut off the stems and tear up spinach. Mix in a glass bowl with:

½ cup red onion, sliced and separated into rings

2 ribs celery, sliced thinly

½ cup pine nuts

½ cup black olives, chopped

Keep salad cold. Whisk together for a dressing:

6 Tbsp. olive oil

2 Tbsp. cider vinegar

½ tsp. salt

½ tsp. dry mustard

Before serving, toss the spinach mixture with the dressing until leaves are coated.

THREE BEAN SALAD

2 cups green beans, French-cut

2 cups red kidney beans

2 cups garbanzo beans

1 green pepper, diced

½ medium onion, diced

⅓ cup sugar

⅓ cup vinegar

½ tsp. salt

Drain the beans well. Place in a glass bowl. Bring to a boil the sugar, vinegar and salt, stirring so sugar is dissolved. Pour over beans. Cover, chill overnight. Stir in diced green pepper and onion. Taste before serving, add a dash of **pepper.**

GREEK SALAD with TOFU

In Greece, this salad would be made with feta cheese, but tofu is a fine non–dairy choice and will absorb the flavors of the dressing.

1 cup tofu, cut in ½″ cubes
5 Tbsp. olive oil
2 Tbsp. vinegar
1 tsp. salt
½ tsp. oregano
½ tsp. basil
¼ tsp. ground bay leaf
1/8 tsp. black pepper

Shake up oil, vinegar and spices in a pint jar. Add tofu cubes and let stand one hour, shaking occasionally. Combine with:

1 cucumber, thinly sliced
red onion, several thin slices
2 tomatoes, cut into wedges
3 cups lettuce, torn up

Toss well and serve garnished with **black olives.**

CABBAGE SLAW

This is best when it's prepared ahead of time.
½ firm head cabbage, shredded (about 6 cups)
1 tsp. salt
2 ribs celery, chopped
2 carrots, grated
Remove outer leaves and core from cabbage. Shred into bowl, toss with the salt, cover and chill for an hour or more. Stir. Add celery and carrots. Mix with *Soymilk Salad Dressing* and let stand. Mix well before serving.

Fruit and Cabbage Salad: Instead of celery and carrots, add **1 small can pineapple tid-bits, 2 sliced bananas** and **2 sliced kiwi** to cabbage. Mix with *Fruit Salad Dressing* (p.154).

SOYMILK SALAD DRESSING

Combine in a blender:
1 small onion (or ¼ cup)
½ cup soymilk
¼ cup oil
¼ cup lemon juice
2 Tbsp. sugar
¼ tsp. salt
Chill or use right away with *Cabbage Slaw.*

PASTA SALAD

Boil **12 ounces** of **rainbow pasta spirals** (about 3½ cups) in boiling salted water until just tender. Drain, run under cold water to cool. Prepare vegetables:

1 green or sweet red pepper, diced
½ cup red onion, chopped
½ cup celery, chopped
1 medium zucchini, diced
¼ cup parsley, minced

Add vegetables to cool pasta, toss well and add enough *Herb Vinaigrette Dressing* to moisten.

HERB VINAIGRETTE DRESSING

Combine in a jar:
⅓ cup cider vinegar
½ tsp. dried basil
1 tsp. salt
1 tsp. oregano or tarragon
½ tsp. dry mustard
¼ cup fresh parsley, minced
¼ tsp. black pepper
½ cup sunflower oil
1 clove garlic, peeled
½ cup olive oil

If you have fresh basil, use twice as much. Combine everything but oils and shake well. Add oils and shake. Discard garlic. Delicious over sliced fresh tomatoes or mixed salad greens.

TOFU SALAD

2 cups tofu
½ cup celery, chopped
2 green onions, chopped
Soymilk Salad Dressing (p.151) or
   Tofu Salad Dressing (p.154)
salt and pepper to taste

Crumble fresh tofu into bowl, or grate it on the coarse side of grater. Add celery, onions and enough salad dressing to moisten. Add salt and pepper to taste.

TEMPUNA SALAD

Steam **8 ounces** of **tempeh** for 15 minutes. Cool. When cold, grate on the coarse side of the grater. Chop **2 stalks celery, 4 green onions** and **¼ cup chopped pickles.**

Mix grated tempeh and vegetables well with:
   ½ cup roasted almonds, chopped
   ½ tsp. salt
   ½ tsp. celery salt
   ¾ cup Tofu Salad Dressing (p.154)
Add **pepper** to taste.

TOFU SALAD DRESSING

Place in blender or processor:
1 cup tofu
¼ cup oil
3 Tbsp. vinegar
1 tsp. honey
½ tsp. salt
Blend until smooth or creamy. For a thinner dressing, add a little water or soymilk. Chill.

THOUSAND ISLAND DRESSING:

Add to *Tofu Salad Dressing:*
¼ cup catsup
½ cup green pepper, chopped
¼ cup onions, chopped

CREAMY ITALIAN DRESSING:

Add to *Tofu Salad Dressing:*
2 garlic cloves, pressed
1 tsp. oregano
¼ tsp. red pepper flakes
Add a little soymilk if dressing is too thick.

FRUIT SALAD DRESSING:

Stir into *Tofu Salad Dressing:*
¼ cup pineapple juice
1 Tbsp. honey
1 Tbsp. celery seed
½ tsp. dry mustard
1 Tbsp. onion, minced (opt.)

Vegetables and Casseroles

HASH BROWNS

Wash and dry **4 potatoes.** Grate, keep potatoes covered with a damp cloth. Put **oil** in the middle of a medium hot skillet, cover with a half inch layer of potatoes. Press flat to hold together as a cake. **Salt** and **pepper** to taste, cover pan. Cook until golden brown on the bottom, then lift a little, add a little oil and turn potatoes to brown the other side.

OVEN FRIED POTATOES

Scrub but don't peel **6 potatoes.** Cut each in half, steam 15−20 minutes until tender. Cool. Put **¼ cup oil** in a large bowl. Cut potatoes in wedges. Add to oil and move around to coat. Place pieces on a cookie sheet. Bake at 450° about 10 minutes, then turn over. Cook 10 minutes more. Sprinkle with **salt** or **nutritional yeast.** Children love these.

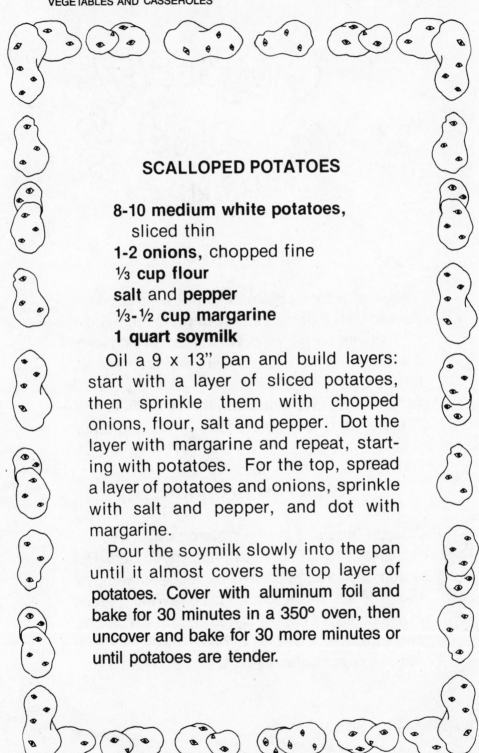

SCALLOPED POTATOES

8-10 medium white potatoes,
sliced thin
1-2 onions, chopped fine
⅓ cup flour
salt and **pepper**
⅓-½ cup margarine
1 quart soymilk

Oil a 9 x 13" pan and build layers: start with a layer of sliced potatoes, then sprinkle them with chopped onions, flour, salt and pepper. Dot the layer with margarine and repeat, starting with potatoes. For the top, spread a layer of potatoes and onions, sprinkle with salt and pepper, and dot with margarine.

Pour the soymilk slowly into the pan until it almost covers the top layer of potatoes. Cover with aluminum foil and bake for 30 minutes in a 350° oven, then uncover and bake for 30 more minutes or until potatoes are tender.

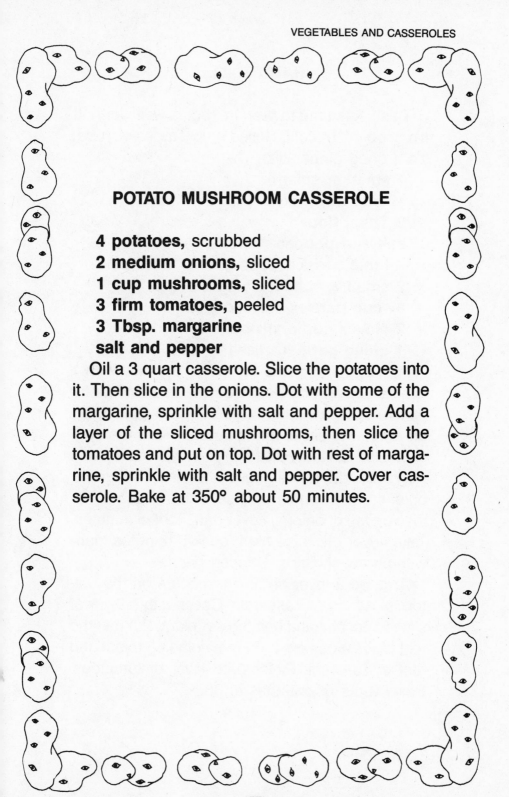

POTATO MUSHROOM CASSEROLE

4 potatoes, scrubbed
2 medium onions, sliced
1 cup mushrooms, sliced
3 firm tomatoes, peeled
3 Tbsp. margarine
salt and pepper

Oil a 3 quart casserole. Slice the potatoes into it. Then slice in the onions. Dot with some of the margarine, sprinkle with salt and pepper. Add a layer of the sliced mushrooms, then slice the tomatoes and put on top. Dot with rest of margarine, sprinkle with salt and pepper. Cover casserole. Bake at 350° about 50 minutes.

RATATOUILLE

This takes time to prepare, but is well worth it. It's good hot or cold. Rolled up in crepes or yuba, it's a good dinner dish.

1 small eggplant
¼ cup olive oil
2 Tbsp. flour
salt and pepper
4 tomatoes, chopped
2 small zucchini
¼ cup parsley, minced
2 cloves garlic, minced
1 green pepper, sliced

Peel eggplant, slice ¼″ thick. Sprinkle with 1 tsp. salt, cover and weight down. Let stand for 30 minutes, prepare other vegies. Drain eggplant, dry on towel, cut slices into quarters. Flour the eggplant pieces. Heat half the oil, fry the eggplant and remove. Add remaining oil to pan, fry garlic, onions and peppers until softened. Place tomatoes on top of onions, cover pan, cook 5 minutes. Take cover off, raise heat, cook 5 minutes more without cover. Stir in minced parsley.

Arrange a layer of tomato mixture on the bottom of a 2 quart casserole. Cover with a layer of sliced zucchini and half the eggplant. Put half the rest of tomatoes on, then remaining eggplant and rest of zucchini. Finish with layer of tomatoes. Bake about 30 minutes at 350°.

VEGETABLE CURRY

Curry powders vary in strength, you can make this mild or hot.

3 potatoes, peeled, cut in quarters
2 carrots, cut in 1" lengths
3 cups water
1 tsp. salt
2 tsp. vegetable bouillon granules
3 Tbsp. oil
1 large onion, cut in wedges
1 large apple, cut in wedges
3 Tbsp. flour
2 tsp. curry powder

Bring the water to a boil, add potatoes, carrots and salt. Cook about 15 minutes until tender. Heat a skillet, add oil and fry onions about 5 minutes to soften. Add apple slices and cook slowly about 10 minutes. Sprinkle flour and curry powder over onions and apples and stir to dissolve. Then slowly add liquid vegetables have cooked in. Add the bouillon granules. Cook and stir until sauce is thick and bubbly. Then add the potatoes and carrots. Serve over hot rice with chutney on the side. This is good made ahead and reheated.

CHINESE FRIED RICE

2 cups frozen tofu, defrosted
2 Tbsp. soy sauce
½ tsp. garlic powder
Press liquid from tofu, cut into small pieces.
Toss with soy sauce and garlic.
Heat a large skillet, fry:
3 Tbsp. oil
2 onions, sliced
2 stalks celery, sliced thinly
When onions soften, add tofu.
Break up and add:
3 cups cold cooked rice
Cook to heat rice. Stir in:
2 Tbsp. soy sauce
½ cup green onions, chopped
Mix well, add bean sprouts if desired.

FRIED GREEN TOMATOES

4 green tomatoes, in ½" slices
½ cup unbleached flour
½ tsp. salt
¼ tsp. pepper
3 Tbsp. oil
Mix flour, salt and pepper on a plate. Heat skillet, add oil. Dredge tomato slices in the seasoned flour. Fry until golden brown.

STUFFED GREEN PEPPERS

3 large green peppers
3 cups rice, cooked
1 large onion, chopped
3 Tbsp. oil
3 cups tomatoes, chopped
1 tsp. each basil and oregano
   (if basil is fresh, use more)
1 tsp. honey

Cut peppers in half lengthwise, remove the seeds. Steam peppers for 5 minutes, turn upside down to drain. Fry the onion lightly in oil. Divide tomatoes in half, reserving half for sauce. Mix the rice, onion, half the tomatoes, spices and add salt and pepper to taste. Stuff shells with mixture, place them in a shallow oiled pan. Puree remaining tomatoes in a blender, adding the honey. Pour over tops of the stuffed peppers. Bake 30–40 minutes at 375º.

JANET'S SAUTEED CABBAGE

Saute a **large onion** in **4 Tbsp. oil** until soft. Cut a good-sized **head of cabbage** into eighths, then slice crosswise. Add cabbage to onions along with:

¾ **tsp. salt**
1 **Tbsp. soy sauce**
1/8 **tsp. pepper**
¼ **tsp. garlic powder**
2 **Tbsp. nutritional yeast flakes** ☆ (opt.)
½ **tsp. vinegar**
2 **Tbsp. oil** (opt.)

Cook over medium high heat, stirring often, till cabbage is soft and golden.

☆ See page 58.

BROCCOLI TOFU STIR FRY

Prepare:
1½ cups broccoli flowerettes
2 carrots, thinly sliced
1½ cups cauliflower pieces
Drop vegetables into **2 cups boiling water.** Boil for 2 minutes, drain, reserve cooking liquid.
Add to liquid for sauce:
3 Tbsp. soy sauce
½ tsp. garlic powder
½ tsp. powdered ginger
1 tsp. sugar
1 Tbsp. cornstarch
In a large skillet or wok, cook a few minutes:
3 Tbsp. oil
2 onions, cut in thin wedges
Add the drained vegetables to the onions, stir. Add:
2 cups tofu, cut in 1″ cubes
Stir in the sauce and cook until sauce is bubbly. Serve on hot rice.

CABBAGE CARROT CASSEROLE

Have ready:
 4 cups green cabbage, sliced thinly
 3 carrots, sliced thinly
 2 onions, sliced
 2 cups Tofu Sour Cream (p.134)
 2 cups bread crumbs ☆
 ¼ cup sesame seeds
Steam the carrot slices until crisp–tender.
Heat in a large pan:
 ¼ cup oil
Add the onions, cook a few minutes, then add cabbage.
 Stir and cook about 10 minutes. Add:
 1 tsp. salt
 ¼ tsp. pepper
Remove from heat and stir in the carrots. Oil an 8″ x 8″ baking pan. Mix half the tofu sour cream into the vegies. Add to remaining tofu **2 Tbsp. nutritional yeast flakes** (p.58). Put this on top of dish. Mix crumbs and seeds and sprinkle on top of casserole. Bake at 350° for 35–40 minutes until top is lightly browned.

☆ Bread crumbs can be made easily by putting 1 or 2 slices of bread at a time in the blender.

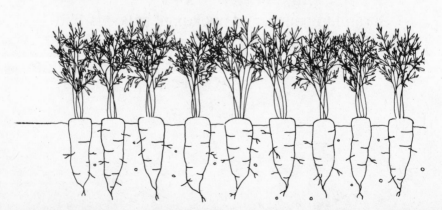

MILLET AND PEAS

Cook until soft:
 1 small onion, chopped
 2 Tbsp. oil
Mix together:
 4 cups boiling water
 2 tsp. vegetable bouillon granules
 1 cup millet
Cook millet until liquid is almost gone. Add:
 2 cups peas, fresh or frozen
 the cooked onions
Cover and let stand 5 or 10 minutes. Stir in:
 ½ cup almonds, slivered

STUFFED MUSHROOMS

12 large mushrooms
½ cup onions, chopped
3 Tbsp. oil
½ cup tofu, crumbled
½ cup bread crumbs
1 Tbsp. nutritional yeast flakes ☆
½ tsp. salt
½ tsp. thyme
½ tsp. garlic powder
 Rinse mushrooms, remove stems. Chop stems.
Fry caps on bottom side a few minutes in 1 Tbsp.
of the oil. Set on oiled baking dish. Fry onions in
the rest of the oil, then fry stems. Mix with tofu,
crumbs and seasonings and stuff caps. Bake at
350° for 15 minutes.

☆ See page 58.

BREAD

Fresh ground flour has more vitamins than any packaged flour you can buy in a store. If you have your own hand grinder, you can buy wheat by the bushel and grind up however much you need of whatever grade flour you like. If you keep the germ in the flour, you must refrigerate it if you're not going to use it right away.

BASIC BREAD-MAKING TIPS

- If the water is too hot it will kill the yeast. If the water isn't hot enough, the yeast won't grow. Slightly warmer than body temperature is good.

- Any sweetener—sugar, honey, molasses, or white potato water—will feed the yeast and make it grow.

- If you double a recipe, you don't have to double the yeast, although you can. The sweetener makes the yeast grow. Your loaves won't rise quite as much when you don't double the yeast.

- Gluten is what makes the dough stick together, and wheat flour has the most gluten. So if you're adding different kinds of flour—rye, corn, barley, soy—add your wheat flour first, stirring it real good, and then add your other flours last.

- Knead bread dough the same way you knead potters clay. Have it in a lump. Draw a piece from the back of the lump towards you, stretching and folding it over towards the front, and push it back into the lump of dough with the palm of your hand. This is to incorporate air into the dough and to develop the gluten. Shift the lump a little with your other hand, moving it in a continuous circular motion after each kneading stroke. Your lump will become a homogenous ball of dough.

- Sometimes if I'm in a hurry, I'll just make the dough into rolls or a loaf, let it rise only once, and then bake it.

BARBARA'S WHOLE WHEAT BREAD

2 loaves

Mix in a large bowl:
 1 cup warm water
 2 Tbsp. baking yeast
 2 Tbsp. sugar or **honey**
Let stand for 10 minutes. Stir in:
 1½ cups warm water
 ¼ cup sugar or **2 Tbsp. honey**
 3 Tbsp. oil
 3 cups white unbleached flour
Whisk until smooth. Let stand for 30 minutes.
Mix in:
 1 tsp. salt
 5–6 cups whole wheat flour
Add enough flour so dough can be turned out
on work surface and kneaded for 5 to 10 minutes.
Put in an oiled bowl, turning to coat dough. Cover
with a damp towel, let rise until double. Oil 2 loaf
pans. Punch down dough and shape into loaves
in pans. Let rise until almost double. Bake in a
preheated 350° oven for 45 to 50 minutes, until
done.

RYE BREAD

2 loaves

1½ cups warm water
2 Tbsp. baking yeast
¼ cup molasses

Sprinkle yeast over water, add molasses.
Let sit 10 minutes, then beat in:

3 cups unbleached white flour
3 cups rye flour
1 tsp. salt
1 Tbsp. caraway seeds

Add enough flour so dough can be kneaded 10 minutes until elastic. Add a small chopped onion if desired. Oil top, cover dough, let rise until doubled. Divide into 2 parts, shape into loaf pans and let rise again until doubled. Preheat oven to 375°. Bake for 40–45 minutes.

HIGH PROTEIN SOY BREAD

2 loaves

Scald **3 cups soymilk.** Pour in bowl and cool to lukewarm. Add to milk:

2 Tbsp. baking yeast
¼ cup oil
1 Tbsp. honey or **sugar**

Let stand for 10 minutes. Whisk in **4 cups unbleached white flour.** Let stand for 20 minutes. Add **2 cups soy flour,** then knead in **3 cups unbleached flour.** Knead for about 10 minutes until smooth. Cover, let rise double. Punch down, shape into 2 loaves, brush tops with oil. Cover, let rise until almost double. Put in oiled loaf pans and bake at 350° about 45 minutes or until golden brown.

Nutrition Notes: This bread is high in protein of a good quality. Wheat and wheat bread don't have enough of the essential amino acid lysine to be a high quality protein. Alone, the protein of wheat and wheat bread is 41% efficient (available to the body). In combination with soymilk and soy flour, the protein of bread is 87% efficient.

There are 6.9 gm. of total protein in each slice of this bread (15 slices per loaf). At 87% efficiency, that is 6 gm. of complete protein per slice. Most other bread, whole wheat or white, contains 2 to 2.4 gm. of total protein per slice, and it is only 41% efficient.

ANADAMA BREAD

2 loaves

Whisk together:
 2 cups boiling water
 ½ cup yellow cornmeal
Stir in:
 ½ cup molasses or **sorghum**
 2 Tbsp. oil
Cool mixture to lukewarm. Combine:
 ½ cup lukewarm water
 2 Tbsp. baking yeast
 1 Tbsp. honey or **sugar**
Let this foam as cornmeal cools. Then add cornmeal mixture to yeast mixture and add: **5 to 6 cups unbleached white flour** to make a stiff dough. Knead 10 minutes. Put dough in an oiled bowl, turning to coat, cover with a damp towel and let rise until double. Punch down with fingertips, cover and let rise again for 45 minutes. Turn out on board and knead again. Oil 2 loaf pans, shape dough into pans, cover and let rise until double. Heat oven to 375° and bake bread for 15 minutes. Reduce heat to 350° and bake 40–45 minutes. Remove from pans while hot, brush tops with oil and let cool on a rack.

SOFT SANDWICH BUNS

Heat **2 cups soymilk** to scalding. Pour into bowl containing:

¼ cup oil
¼ cup sugar

Let mixture cool. In a large bowl, place:

2 Tbsp. yeast
1 tsp. sugar
¼ cup warm water

Let yeast mixture sit a few minutes, then add the cooled milk. Whisk in **2 cups white unbleached flour** and beat 100 times until smooth. Let sponge rest 10 minutes. Beat in **4 cups flour** and **1 tsp. salt.** Add enough flour so dough can be turned out to knead 5 minutes. Shape rolls, put on oiled cookie sheet. Let rise 30 minutes. Heat oven to 375° and bake rolls about 20 minutes. You can make breadsticks, sopapillas, fancy rolls or doughnuts from this same dough.

BREADSTICKS

One recipe of *Soft Sandwich Buns* will make 4 or 5 dozen bread sticks. After first rise, punch dough down, break off pieces and roll between your palms into a stick ½″ thick and 5 or 6 inches long. Roll sticks in poppy seeds, sesame seeds or caraway seeds. Put on oiled cookie sheets a ½″ apart. Cover, let rise almost double.

Preheat oven to 400°. Bake 6 minutes and use tongs to turn sticks over. Bake 7 to 10 minutes more, until golden brown. These will get crunchier as they cool.

SOPAPILLAS
("Little Pillows")

Use one–half of the *Soft Sandwich Bun* recipe. Roll it out to 1/8 inch thick. Cut into diamond or triangular shapes. Let rise 30 minutes. Fry in deep fat until golden brown on one side, turn over and fry other side. Fill these with jam and roll in sugar or fill with mashed beans and roll in nutritional yeast flakes (p.58).

CINNAMON ROLLS

After *Soft Sandwich Bun* dough has risen, divide into two balls. Roll each out into a long rectangle. Spread with **½ cup brown sugar** mixed with **1 tsp. cinnamon.** Add ½ cup raisins (opt.) and dot with a little margarine if desired. Roll up like a jelly roll and cut with a sharp knife into 1″ slices. Put on an oiled cookie sheet and let rise nearly double. Preheat oven to 400° degrees and bake about 15 minutes. Glaze tops with: **½ cup powdered sugar** mixed with **1 Tbsp. lemon juice.**

PECAN ROLLS

Make *Soft Sandwich Bun* dough. While dough is rising, cut up **1 cup pecans.** Oil well 2 dozen muffin tins, sprinkle the bottom of each with a little **brown sugar** and dots of **margarine.** Put pecans in bottoms of tins. Roll out dough, put a little brown sugar and dots of margarine on, roll up like a jelly roll and cut into 24 slices. Place a slice in each muffin tin, cover and let rise until nearly double. Preheat oven to 400° and bake 12 to 15 minutes. Turn out at once as bottoms will be sticky, or lift rolls out with a big spoon, turn upside down to cool.

QUICK ITALIAN BREAD
(One of our kids' favorites)

Combine in a large bowl:

3 cups warm water
2 Tbsp. baking yeast
2 Tbsp. sugar
2 Tbsp. oil

Let sit 5 minutes. Whip in **4 cups unbleached flour,** then stir in **5 more cups flour** and **1 tsp. salt.** Do not knead. Cover, let rise until double. Punch down and make two balls. Flaten each ball and roll into a long loaf. Dust cookie sheet with cornmeal. Put loaves on sheet, slash tops in 3 places. Let rise 30 minutes. Put a 9″ x 13″ pan of boiling water on the bottom of a cold oven. Put loaves in oven, turn it on to 400° and bake 35–45 minutes. Brush margarine on tops. Spread leftover bread slices with margarine, sprinkle with garlic powder and broil until brown.

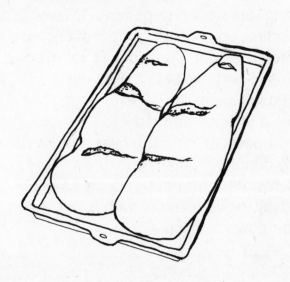

SERGE'S FRENCH BREAD

Makes 3 small loaves

8½ cups flour
2½ cups cold water
50 mg. ascorbic acid
 (vitamin C)
¼ cup warm water
2-3 Tbsp. yeast
2 tsp. sugar
2 tsp. salt

Mix flour, water and vitamin C in a bowl. Knead for 15 minutes. Dissolve yeast and sugar in warm water. Knead yeast mixture into dough till well mixed.

Knead salt into the dough for 10 minutes. Let bread rise 20 minutes. Preheat oven to 400° and put a pan of boiling water at the bottom.

Shape bread into loaves. Make 3 slits on top of each loaf, 3" long and not very deep. Bake till brown, about 30 minutes. Brush on **margarine.**

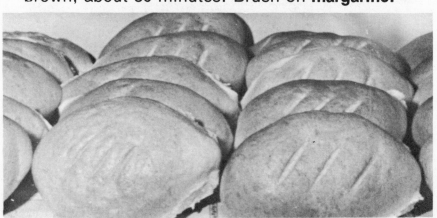

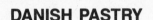

DANISH PASTRY

Cream together: **1 cup margarine** and **1 cup white unbleached flour.** Pat into a a 5″ x 9″ rectangle on waxed paper. Chill 30 minutes or more. In a large bowl, place **2 Tbsp. yeast, 2 Tbsp. sugar, 2 cups warm water.** Let stand 10 minutes. Whisk in **1 tsp. lemon juice, ½ tsp. cardamon** and **¼ cup sugar.** Whisk until free of lumps, cover, let rise 20 minutes. Stir in **½ tsp. salt** and **4½ cups of unbleached flour.** Turn dough out and knead until elastic. Roll out to a ½ inch thick rectangle. Place the margarine and flour mixture on one side, fold the dough over to encase it. Pound lightly, then fold over in thirds. Roll out to 1″ thick, fold in thirds, roll again. Repeat fold and roll 3 more times. If the margarine begins to ooze out, chill dough. Divide in half.

Dough keeps overnight chilled. You can make one large Danish and 24 croissants. Roll dough out size of a cookie sheet. Fold and lift onto oiled sheet. Open flat, spoon filling down center. Use *Tofu Whipped Topping* (p.101), *Yogurt Cream Cheese* (p.110) or fruit. With a sharp knife, cut slits 1″ apart from outer edge to filling. Braid strips over filling. Lightly oil top of dough and let rise 45 minutes. Preheat oven to 375°. Bake 25–30 minutes. Cool. Glaze top with: **½ cup powdered sugar** mixed with **1 Tbsp. lemon juice.**

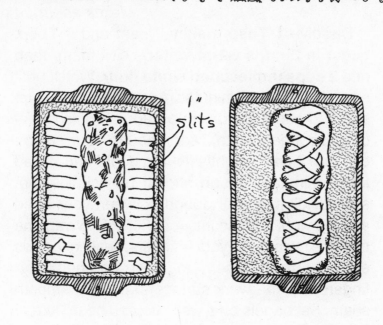

Croissants

Divide remaining dough (it will keep overnight in refrigerator) into 2 balls. Roll out each ball into a large circle. Cut into 12 triangles. Roll each triangle up, starting from the wide base, tucking tip under to seal. Place on oiled cookie sheets, shaping each roll into a crescent. Let rise almost double. Preheat oven to 375°. Bake until golden brown, about 20 minutes. Makes 2 dozen flaky rolls.

JANET'S BAGELS

Makes about 24

Dissolve **1 Tbsp. baking yeast** and **2 Tbsp. sugar** in **2 cups warm water.** Let it foam, then add **2 cups unbleached white flour.** Whisk until smooth, let rise 10 minutes. Add ½ **cup oil, 1 tsp. salt** and about **4 more cups flour** (whole wheat or unbleached white). Add enough flour so you can turn it onto a lightly floured board and knead for l0 minutes. Dough should be soft, but not sticky. Roll lumps of dough between your hand and the work surface into rolls ¾" x 8". Wrap one end of a roll around your 4 fingers, sealing the two ends by rolling them together between your fingers and the work surface to make a smooth seam. Set bagels on a well–floured board to rise for 5 to 10 minutes.

Have ready a 4 quart pot two–thirds full of boiling water. Add **2 Tbsp. sugar** to water. Drop 4 or 5 bagels into the rapidly boiling water, risen side down, and cover the pan. Boil 30 seconds on one side, turn over, boil 30 seconds on the other side, keeping water at a rapid boil. Remove bagels with a slotted spoon and place on an oiled cookie sheet. Bake them in a preheated oven at 375° for 25–30 minutes or until golden brown. Cool on a rack.

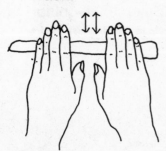

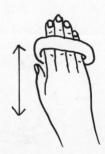

quick breads

JANIE'S GOOD BISCUITS

4 cups unbleached flour
3½ tsp. baking powder
1 tsp. salt
1¾ cups soymilk
¼ cup oil

Sift dry ingredients together. You can use part whole wheat, part buckwheat or all white. Make a well in center, add milk and oil. Stir enough to moisten, turn onto a floured surface and knead a few minutes. Roll to ½″ thick, cut with a 2″ cutter or tin can. (A bigger cut will rise less). Put close together on an oiled cookie sheet. Heat oven to 450°, bake 10–15 minutes until browned on bottom. You can use sour milk in these, substitute ½ tsp. soda for 1 tsp. of the baking powder.

SCONES

Add ¼ **cup sugar** to dry ingredients above, and stir in **1 cup raisins** or **currants.** Divide dough in half. Roll each half into a ½″ thick circle and cut dough into wedges. Bake as directed above.

SKILLET CORN BREAD

8 wedges

1½ cups cornmeal
1½ cups unbleached white flour
3½ tsp. baking powder
1 Tbsp. sugar or **honey**
1 tsp. salt
2¼ cups soymilk or **water**
¼ cup oil

Heat oven to 400°. Put an oiled 10″ iron skillet in oven to heat. Mix the dry ingredients well, stir in the milk and oil. You can use sour milk, but use 1 tsp. baking soda instead of 1 tsp. baking powder. Pour into the hot skillet and bake 30 minutes on the top shelf. You can run it under the broiler for a browner top. Cut into wedges and serve hot from the oven (or take out of the pan and reheat later).

Mexican Cornbread: Add to batter: **1 small onion,** chopped; **2 cups whole kernel corn, 2 tsp. chili powder.** Bake as directed above and serve hot.

BOSTON BROWN BREAD

3 cans

Have 3 cans ready, about 4″ in diameter and 5 or 6 inches high. Oil cans well and cut a circle of waxed paper to fit in bottom of each.

1 cup unbleached white flour
1 cup whole wheat flour
1 cup cornmeal
2 tsp. baking soda
1 tsp. salt
¾ cup raisins
½ cup molasses or **sorghum**
2 cups sour milk

Sift together the flours, baking soda and salt. Add the cornmeal and raisins. Stir to mix well. Stir in the molasses and sour milk. Fill the well−oiled cans ⅔ full. Cover cans with foil and tie on tightly. Place on rack in steamer and steam for 2½ to 3 hours. Check to be sure the water level remains half way up the cans.

BANANA BREAD

Sift together:
 2 cups unbleached white flour
 1½ tsp. baking powder
 ½ tsp. baking soda
Cream until light and fluffy:
 ⅓ cup margarine
 ¾ cup brown sugar
Beat into sugar mixture:
 1 cup bananas, mashed (about 2)
Mix together:
 3 Tbsp. soymilk or **water**
 1 tsp. vanilla
Add liquids to banana mixture, then stir in the sifted flour. Fold in ½ cup chopped nuts if desired. Preheat oven to 350". Pour dough into oiled loaf pan. Bake 45–50 minutes.

COFFEE CAKE

Sift together:
  3 cups unbleached flour
  1 cup sugar
  1 tsp. cinnamon
  ¾ tsp. nutmeg
  ½ tsp. allspice
Cut in **¾ cup margarine** (1½ sticks). Set aside
1 cup of this mixture for topping.
  Add to rest of flour mixture:
  1¼ cups soymilk
  3 tsp. baking powder
  ½ cup raisins (opt.)
Mix well, pour into an oiled 8″ x 8″ pan. Sprinkle with the topping mixture. Add **½ cup** of
chopped walnuts to topping if desired. Preheat
oven to 375°. Bake for 25–30 minutes, until a knife
inserted in center comes out clean.

A high protein cold cereal

Mix together:

3 cups rolled oats
1 cup wheat germ
1 cup sunflower seeds, lightly toasted
¼ cup soy powder or **soy pulp**
½ cup coconut

Heat together and stir into oat mixture:

½ cup honey ☆
½ cup oil
1 tsp. vanilla

Spread out evenly on 2 cookie sheets. Bake at 325° for 30 minutes or until golden. Turn with a pancake turner a few times so it browns evenly. Cool. Stir in **raisins** or cut up **dried apples** or **apricots.** Store in an airtight container.

☆Or use 1 cup brown sugar heated with ½ cup hot water and the oil.

Nutrition Notes: There are 14.6 gm. of protein per cup of Granola. 82% of this protein is complete. ¾ cup of Granola and ½ cup of soymilk provides 15 gm. of complete protein.

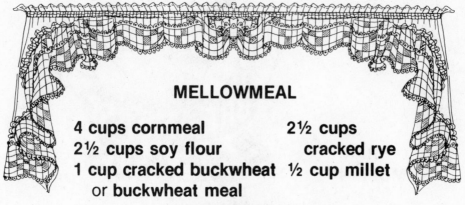

MELLOWMEAL

4 cups cornmeal   2½ cups
2½ cups soy flour   cracked rye
1 cup cracked buckwheat ½ cup millet
   or buckwheat meal

FARMOLA

2 cups cracked wheat 1 cup cornmeal
   or cream of wheat   1 cup soy flour
1 cup cracked rye

Farmola and Mellowmeal are balanced high-protein breakfast cereals. Both must be thoroughly cooked to make the soy flour and grain digestible. Combine the ingredients well and store in airtight containers.

Whisk 1 part of either cereal into **3 parts salted boiling water.** Stir the cereal constantly while it is first thickening. Then reduce heat and cook for a good 25 minutes, stirring often. Serve hot with soymilk, sugar, sorghum, molasses, margarine, or just plain with salt.

Variation: Toast cereal in a cast iron skillet over medium heat, stirring constantly with a wooden spoon, until grains are browned and have a nutlike aroma. Then cook as above.

Nutrition Notes: There are 20.8 gm. of protein per cup of uncooked Mellowmeal; 95% of this protein is complete. There are 26 gm. of protein per cup of uncooked Farmola; 75% of this protein is complete.

BRAN MUFFINS

2 cups unbleached flour
1 cup bran or wheat germ
1½ tsp. baking soda
½ tsp. salt
2 cups sour soymilk or yogurt
⅓ cup honey or sorghum
¼ cup oil
½ cup raisins

Stir dry ingredients together and make a well in the middle. Pour in the liquid ingredients and raisins. Stir just enough to moisten flour. Spoon into 12 large well-oiled muffin tins. Bake at 425° for 18–20 minutes.

FRENCH TOAST

Mix together with a whisk:
1 cup soymilk
2 Tbsp. flour
1 tsp. sugar
1 Tbsp. nutritional yeast flakes ☆
½ tsp. salt

Dip slices of bread into the mixture to coat well. Heat oil in a skillet and fry slices until golden brown and crispy on both sides. Serve hot with cinnamon and honey or syrup.

☆See page 58.

PANCAKES

Sift together:
1¼ cups flour
2 Tbsp. sugar
2 tsp. baking powder
½ tsp. salt

Mix together:
2 Tbsp. oil
1¼ cups water or
½ cup soymilk
+ ¾ cup water

Make a hole in the center of the dry ingredients. Pour the wet mixture into the dry and mix with a wooden spoon only until ingredients are blended. The batter should be somewhat lumpy, which makes the cakes light. If you beat the batter smooth, the pancakes will be tough.

You can try replacing 2 Tbsp. of flour with 2 Tbsp. of cornmeal when mixing the dry ingredients. If you use whole wheat flour instead of white, the batter may need more liquid. It should be thin enough to pour.

Heat your griddle over a medium high flame. It's hot enough when water dropped on it turns to beads and bounces across the griddle. Then oil griddle slightly. Pour cakes and flip them when tops bubble up. You may need to lower the flame a little to keep pancakes from burning, but the higher the flame, the lighter the pancakes.

Waffles: Cut liquid in half and bake in a preheated waffle iron.

OLD-TIME BUCKWHEAT CAKES
Makes about 36, 6" in diameter

1 cake or 1 Tbsp. dry yeast
½ cup lukewarm water
2 cups cold water
1 cup flour, white or whole wheat
   (white's best)
2 cups buckwheat flour
1½ tsp. salt
1 Tbsp. molasses
1 tsp. soda
½ cup hot water
4 Tbsp. margarine

Dissolve yeast in lukewarm water. Then add cold water. Sift flour once before measuring. Then sift flour, buckwheat flour and salt together. Blend yeast mixture into the flour mixture. Beat vigorously until the batter is smooth. Cover and let stand overnight.

In the morning, blend in molasses, soda dissolved in ½ cup hot water and 4 Tbsp. melted margarine. Let stand at room temperature for 30 minutes. Drop mixture from tip of spoon onto lightly oiled hot griddle. Cook on one side. When puffed full of bubbles and cooked on edges, turn and cook on other side. Do not mash down.

Note: To use batter as a starter for another batch of buckwheat cakes, save out 1 cup of batter (before adding molasses and soda), add 1 cup of cold water, cover and place in refrigerator until the night before you wish to use it. Pour off water which has risen to the top of batter. Blend in same amount of flour, buckwheat flour and salt as in original recipe. Add 2½ cups cold water, cover and let stand overnight. In the morning, follow directions for adding soda and molasses as in the original recipe.

Variation: This recipe can also be used for making white flour or whole wheat flour pancakes.

MARNA'S GOOD GRIDDLE CAKES

Sift together:
  2 cups buckwheat flour
  2 cups cornmeal
  1½ tsp. salt
  1 Tbsp. baking powder
  2 Tbsp. sugar (opt.)
Add to dry ingredients:
  about 2 cups soymilk or **water**
  1 Tbsp. melted margarine

Mix together—don't worry about stirring out all the lumps. Just add enough until you have a batter than can be easily managed on the griddle. Your griddle is ready to fry when a few drops of water dance across the surface.

Serve them hot with margarine and syrup, or spread with jelly and roll 'em up.

APPLE COBBLER

Peel, core and slice:

6 large apples

Melt in a large skillet:

3 Tbsp. margarine

Cook apples over low heat for 5 minutes, then sprinkle them with:

3 Tbsp. sugar

1 tsp. cinnamon

Continue to cook apples 10 minutes more. Remove from heat.

Batter:

Combine:

1½ cups unbleached flour

½ cup sugar

1½ tsp. baking powder

Stir dry ingredients together, then add:

¼ cup oil

1 cup soymilk

1 tsp. vanilla

Mix together. Arrange a layer of batter in an oiled 8″ x 8″ pan, arrange the apple slices on top. Spoon remaining batter over apples. Bake cobbler at 350° about 25 minutes.

Blueberry Cobbler: Rinse **1 to 2 cups blueberries,** sprinkle with **sugar** to taste. Make batter as above, add berries. Pour into 8″ x 8″ pan and bake as above.

BLINTZES

Combine:

1 cup white flour   **1 Tbsp. sugar**
¼ cup oat flour   **1 tsp. baking powder**
½ tsp. salt

Whisk in **4 cups cold water.** Pour 1/8-1/4 cup batter in a hot, lightly oiled frying pan and immediately tilt the pan to spread the batter evenly over the surface of the pan in about 6" circles. They should be real thin like crepes. Cook only on one side till the top side is dry and has bubbles on it. Stack the blintzes inside a folded cloth.

Filling:

2 cups pressed tofu
6 Tbsp. margarine, melted
½ cup soy sour cream or **blended tofu**
6 Tbsp. sugar   **½ tsp. salt**

Place 3 Tbsp. filling in the middle of the cooked side of each blintze. Fold the two ends toward the middle, then fold the remaining sides over each other. Place on a cookie sheet with folded side down. When ready to serve, fry each blintze in **margarine** till crisp and golden.

Serve with *Tofu Sour Cream* (p.134) or fruit sauce, or serve plain.

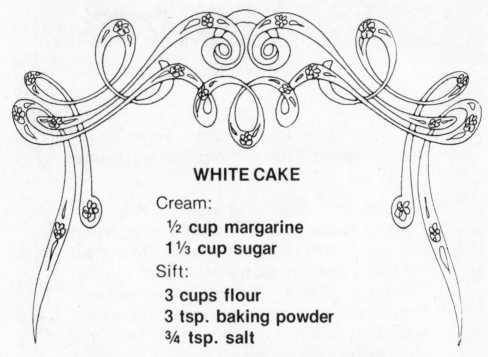

WHITE CAKE

Cream:

 ½ cup margarine
 1⅓ cup sugar

Sift:

 3 cups flour
 3 tsp. baking powder
 ¾ tsp. salt

Mix dry ingredients into creamed mixture alternately with **2 cups liquid** (soymilk or water). Add **1 Tbsp. vanilla.** Beat 2 minutes. Bake in a 9 x 13" pan at 350° for 30 minutes.

Variation: The liquid can be replaced with **2 cups soy yogurt** (p.108) or **whey** (from making tofu, p.116); replace baking powder with **1½ tsp. baking powder** and **½ tsp. baking soda.** Bake as above.

For Marble Cake:

Pour ⅔ of the *White Cake* batter into cake pan. Dissolve **¼ cup cocoa** in **4 Tbsp. melted margarine** (slightly cooled) and beat until smooth. Add to the remaining ⅓ batter, along with ⅓ **cup sugar.** Beat till smooth. Spoon the chocolate cake batter on top of white batter in pan and swirl with a knife or spatula. Bake as for *White Cake.*

FLUFFY ICING
for a 9 x 13" cake

Combine in a medium saucepan with a whisk:

1 cup cold water
5 Tbsp. flour

Cook over medium heat, whisking constantly until very thick and smooth. Be careful not to burn. Cool completely by setting in a pan of cold water.

Cream until sandy:

1 cup sugar
3-6 Tbsp. margarine
1 tsp. vanilla
pinch of salt
3 Tbsp. cocoa (opt.)

Whip the creamed mixture into the cool flour mixture until well blended and fluffy, then spread on the cake.

If the frosting separates, reheat it while whipping constantly, then refrigerate until cool.

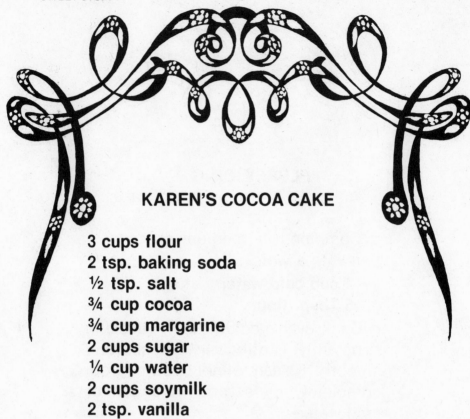

KAREN'S COCOA CAKE

3 cups flour
2 tsp. baking soda
½ tsp. salt
¾ cup cocoa
¾ cup margarine
2 cups sugar
¼ cup water
2 cups soymilk
2 tsp. vanilla

Sift together the flour, soda, salt and cocoa. Set this aside while you cream the margarine. Gradually cream in the sugar. Add the water and beat well.

Add the flour mixture alternately with the milk. Add vanilla and beat well.

Oil and flour a 9 x 13" pan. Pour in the batter. Bake at 350° for about 45 minutes or until a toothpick comes out clean when you poke the center.

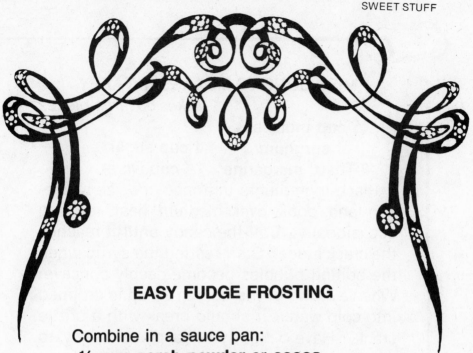

EASY FUDGE FROSTING

Combine in a sauce pan:
   ⅓ cup carob powder or **cocoa**
   ⅓ cup soy milk or **water**
Bring to a rolling boil. Remove from heat, add:
   1 Tbsp. margarine
   1 tsp. vanilla
Cool a little, then quickly stir in:
   2 cups powdered sugar
Spread on cake while frosting is warm. If it begins to harden add a little water.

MISS DORSA'S MOLASSES TAFFY
Makes 50 large pieces

⅔ cup molasses
or **sorghum**   **1 cup sugar**
3 Tbsp. margarine   ⅔ cup water

Place ingredients in a medium-size saucepan and cook over medium heat, stirring occasionally. Boil the candy until it reaches the crack stage. Start testing the syrup when the boiling bubbles become deeply concave. When a string of the boiling syrup is dropped into cold water, it should break with a brittle crack. Have a lightly oiled platter ready to pour the candy onto when it reaches the crack stage. You may have to test the boiling syrup several times. Change the water for each test.

When it reaches the crack stage, remove from heat immediately and pour onto the prepared platter. Let it cool just long enough to be able to pick it up and pull it without burning your fingers. It should still be fairly warm and hold together in one piece. Oil your fingers and start pulling the taffy, using just your fingertips and holding it very lightly to allow maximum aeration. It is the air added while the taffy is being pulled that turns it from a dark molasses color to a light golden color. The taffy is done when it gets light and golden and too hard to pull smoothly and rapidly, usually in 10-15 minutes of pulling.

At this point stretch it out into a long even rope and lay it out on a lightly oiled cookie sheet to finish cooling. Cool 10-15 minutes or until the taffy breaks evenly when held in the palm of your hand and struck sharply with the handle of a knife. This may take some practice. Hold the strand of taffy so your hand forms a hollow beneath where you strike with the knife handle. If taffy is undercooked it will be too soft to break and may be cut into bite-size pieces.

BROWNIES

Mix ⅓ **cup flour** with **1 cup water**. Cook until thick and cool completely.

Melt ½ **cup margarine**. Add ⅔ **cup cocoa** and stir until smooth. Cool.

Beat **2 cups sugar, ½ tsp. salt,** and **1 tsp. vanilla** into the cooled flour mixture, then add cocoa mixture.

Mix together **2 cups flour** and **2½ tsp. baking powder** and add to above ingredients. You can add ½ **cup chopped walnuts** or pecans. Bake in an oiled 9″ x 13″ pan at 350° for 20 to 25 minutes.

Fudge Brownies: Decrease the flour to **1½ cups** and the baking powder to **1½ tsp.**

SWEET POTATO PIE

2 cups sweet potatoes, pumpkin or
butternut squash, mashed
1 cup soymilk
¾ cup brown sugar or **½ cup honey**
1 Tbsp. molasses
½ tsp. salt   **3 Tbsp. oil**
½ tsp. nutmeg   **1 tsp. cinnamon**
½ tsp. powdered ginger
¼ tsp. powdered cloves
¼ cup cornstarch

Mix cooked mashed vegetable with milk and sugar. Add oil and molasses. Mix the cornstarch with the spices and stir in. Pour into an unbaked pie shell. Bake in a hot oven (425°) for 10 minutes, then reduce heat to 350° and bake 40 to 50 minutes until filling is set in the middle. Serve with *Tofu Whipped Topping* (p.101).

LOUISE'S GINGERBREAD

Makes one 8 x 8" pan

1 cup sorghum or **molasses**
½ cup melted margarine or **oil**
2 tsp. ginger
2 cups flour
1 tsp. salt
1 tsp. soda
  in **1 cup hot water**

Beat together molasses and margarine, then beat in flour, ginger and salt. Beat in soda water about ⅓ cup at a time, till mixture is smooth. Bake at 350° for 35-40 minutes.

HONEYCAKE

Makes one 9" round pan

1 cup honey
¼ cup water
2 cups rye flour
1 tsp. cinnamon
½ tsp. allspice
¼ tsp. mace
2 tsp. baking powder
½ cup chopped nuts

Blend in honey and water, then beat in dry ingredients and blend in nuts. Bake at 350° with a pan of boiling water on the bottom of the oven for about 40 minutes.

Let the cake age in plastic or a tin box for a few days before eating.

APPLESAUCE CAKE

½ cup oil
1 cup sugar
2 cups unbleached flour
2 cups applesauce
1½ tsp. baking soda
1 tsp. cinnamon
½ tsp. nutmeg
½ tsp. vanilla
½ cup raisins (opt.)

Mix oil and sugar well, add applesauce, and mix in the dry ingredients. Beat until smooth. Pour in an oiled and floured 9″ x 13″ pan and bake at 350° for 30–35 minutes, or into an oiled loaf pan and bake for 45–50 minutes until done. This cake is even better the next day.

CARROT CAKE

Preheat oven to 350°.

1 cup salad oil
1 cup white sugar + 1 cup brown sugar
  or **2 cups brown sugar**
1½ cups water or **soymilk**
4 cups unbleached white flour
2 tsp. baking powder
2 tsp. baking soda
1 tsp. salt
1½ tsp. cinnamon
½ tsp. allspice
3 cups grated raw carrots
1 cup chopped nuts (opt.)
½ cup raisins (opt.)

Blend oil and sugar, add water and beat. Sift the flour with remaining ingredients and add to sugar mixture. Add carrots and nuts and mix well. Bake in 3 oiled and floured layer pans or one 9 x 13" cake pan at 350° for 35-40 minutes. (Baking time may be less if using small round pans.)

BREAD PUDDING

Serves 4-6

Mix together well:
3½ cups soymilk
⅔ cup sugar
½ tsp. salt
1 Tbsp. vanilla
1 tsp. cinnamon

Pour this over **4 cups of old bread** broken up into bite-size pieces in a square baking pan. Dot the top with ¼ **cup margarine.** Bake for 20 minutes at 350°.

CAROB-CAROB CHIP BARS

Combine in a saucepan:
¼ cup flour
½ cup water
Cook and stir until thick. Cool.
Blend until smooth:

½ cup tofu	**1 cup sugar**
¼ cup oil	**1 tsp. vanilla**
¼ cup water	

Mix together:
¾ cup flour
1 tsp. baking powder
½ cup carob powder
Add the flour and water paste to tofu mixture, then stir in the dry ingredients. Last, stir in **1 cup carob chips.** Add **½ cup chopped walnuts or pecans** if desired. Put into an oiled 8″ x 8″ pan. Bake at 350° for 25 minutes. Cool. Cut into 12 bars.

Mint Carob Chip Bars: For minty carob bars, use **½ tsp. peppermint flavoring** instead of vanilla.

WALNUT BALLS

½ cup soft margarine
2 Tbsp. sugar
1 t. vanilla
1 cup walnuts, chopped small
1 cup unbeached flour
Mix together and shape into 30 small balls. Place on lightly oiled baking sheet. Bake for 20-25 minutes at 350°.

CHOCOLATE CHIP COOKIES

Makes 6 dozen

2½ cups flour
1½ tsp. baking powder
½ tsp. salt
½ cup brown sugar
½ cup white sugar
½ cup oil
¼ cup water
1 tsp. vanilla
1 cup chocolate chips

Sift flour, baking powder, and salt. Mix sugars and stir in oil. Add water and vanilla and beat till blended. Add dry ingredients to creamed mixture and mix well. Add chocolate chips, mix well. Drop by teaspoons on oiled cookie sheets. Bake at 350° for 15 minutes or until golden on the bottom.

PEANUT BUTTER COOKIES

Cream together:
1 cup peanut butter
½ cup margarine
1 cup honey
½ tsp. vanilla

Sift and add:
2 cups flour
½ tsp. salt
2 tsp. baking powder

Roll into little balls. Place on an oiled cookie sheet and flatten with a fork which has been dipped in oil or water.

Bake at 375° for 15 minutes.

OATMEAL COOKIES

Makes about 5 dozen

½ cup margarine
⅓ cup oil
1 cup brown sugar, packed
1 cup white sugar
⅓ cup soymilk
2 tsp. vanilla
2½ cups flour
1 tsp. baking powder
1 tsp. baking soda
1 tsp. salt
3 cups rolled oats
½ cup raisins (opt.)

Cream margarine and oil together, then cream in the sugars. Add soymilk and vanilla. Beat until smooth. Beat in flour, baking powder, soda and salt. Mix, add oats and raisins and blend in well. Bake at 350° for about 15 minutes or until the undersides just start turning brown.

NUTRITION NOTES

Vegetarian nutrition is pretty similar to conventional nutrition except in the special areas of protein, vitamin B12, and the feeding of small children. Most nutrients come from standard sources: vitamin A from dark green vegetables, yellow root vegetables, some yellow fruits, and fortified margarine; vitamin C from dark leafy greens and citrus (also potatoes, cauliflower, sweet potatoes, and broccoli). Iron is abundant in legumes and greens; calcium in grains, greens, and soybeans; and the B vitamins in whole grains, potatoes, nutritional yeast, fortified breads and flours, and many fresh vegetables.

Soybeans are a very important food, supplying protein, iron, B vitamins, and calcium.

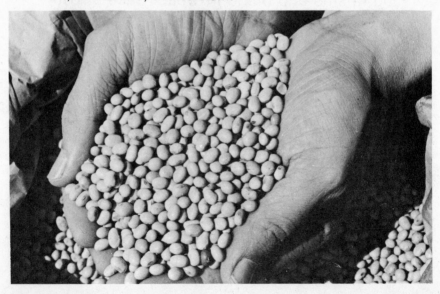

Protein for Complete Vegetarians

The word *protein* comes from the Greek word *proteios* which means *primary*. You are mostly made of protein except for water and the mineral portions of bones. It forms the muscles and skin, hair and nails, the hemoglobin of the blood which carries oxygen to the body; it forms enzymes and most hormones which regulate the metabolism and functions of the body; it helps maintain the fluid balance of the body and acts as a buffer for acid and base; and it forms the antibodies which protect you from unfriendly microorganisms.

Protein is made up of smaller units called amino acids. There are 22 amino acids. In different combinations and different numbers, they make up the different proteins of the body. Fats, carbohydrates and proteins are all made of carbon, oxygen and hydrogen, but protein contains the added element of nitrogen (and sometimes sulfur). Your body can synthesize most of the amino acids. These are called the *non-essential amino acids.* The amino acids which cannot be synthesized by the body from nitrogen and other substances containing carbon, oxygen and hydrogen are called *essential amino acids.* There are eight of them: tryptophan, threonine, isoleucine, leucine, lysine, methionine, phenylalanine, and valine. A ninth, histidine, is essential to babies for growth.

The body's own protein is constantly being broken down into amino acids and resynthesized back into proteins. These amino acids are not different from those obtained from food. Together they form the amino acid pool that services the body. Some nitrogen is always being excreted and some is always being added by eating. New amino acids are needed to replace those already present and to form new protein for growth and healing. If the nitrogen lost is the same amount as the nitrogen gained, the body is in "nitrogen balance." Growing children and pregnant and nursing ladies should be in "positive nitrogen balance"—that is, more gained than lost.

The function of protein is mainly to provide for tissue growth and repair, but if the carbohydrate and fat intake (calories) is inadequate, it will be used for fuel. Carbohydrates and fats are called "protein-sparing" because they leave the protein for its own special functions.

When you eat the protein of plants, which they make from the nitrogen of the soil and air, it's absorbed as amino acids and resynthesized as protein in the tissues. To resynthesize in the tissues, the essential amino acids need to be in a specific ratio. If an essential amino acid is missing, the other essential amino acids that would make up the complete protein in the tissues are unusable as such and are broken down into fats or sugars (certain ones go to fat and certain ones to sugar), and the nitrogen is lost as urea or goes to form non-essential amino acids. If a certain amino acid is lower in proportion to the others than it should be, the protein will resynthesize in the tissues up to the level of the *limiting amino acid* (or acids) and the remaining ones that are incomplete will break down.

Vegetable Sources of High Quality Proteins

Soybeans and soy products such as soymilk, tofu, yogurt, and tempeh have within them a *complete* protein. All the essential amino acids are present and in the right proportions, and their protein is as growth-promoting as that of meat or dairy products.

There is also high quality protein in wheat germ, oats, garbanzo beans, sunflower seeds, buckwheat (kasha), red, white and black beans, rice, peanuts, pumpkin seeds and cashews. These are foods whose *limiting amino acid* reaches at least 70% of that of an *ideal protein.* * In other words, 70% of the protein within the food is complete. The remainder of the protein can be made complete by combining the food with another food which is high in the limiting amino acid.

In plants, the usual limiting essential amino acids are lysine, methionine, and tryptophan. (Since another amino acid called cystine can be converted to methionine, these two can be grouped together as the "sulfur-containing amino acids," or S.C.) The limiting amino acid in grains, seeds, and nuts is lysine. The sulfur-containing amino acids are limiting in beans. Tryptophan is limiting in some grains and in some beans.

So, when combining plant proteins for optimum quality, the basic combination is beans served with grains, nuts or seeds. Grains also combine well with nutritional yeast. Soybeans and soy products do not need to be combined as they are complete in themselves. But soymilk or a little tofu added to any meal will boost its protein quality and quantity.

There is also high quality protein in many fresh vegetables. But the quantity of protein is not high like grains or beans. However, if large amounts of the following vegetables are eaten, they can contribute substantially to the protein requirements: green beans, swiss chard, broccoli, mustard greens, asparagus, and potatoes.

*Amino Acid Pattern for High Quality Proteins in *Recommended Dietary Allowances,* 8th Revised Edition. Food and Nutrition Board, National Research Council. National Academy of Sciences, Washington, D.C. 1974, page 4.

A WORD

If you are a complete vegetarian, eating only plant food, you will need to supplement vitamin B12. This vitamin does not occur in the vegetable kingdom, and a lack of it can cause severe nervous system damage. The basic source of B12 in nature is synthesis by micro-organisms. (It is synthesized by intestinal flora but most people are unable to absorb it because it is produced in a lower part of the intestine than where it must be absorbed.)

Crystalline B12 is obtained from synthesis by *Streptomyces griseus* (the micro-organism that produces *streptomycin*). Some brands of nutritional yeast and TVP contain added B12. It does not occur naturally in yeast or yogurt. A tiny bit of B12 is produced by the bacteria that ferment miso. But you would have to eat 2 cups of miso a day to get 1 mcg. of B12.

In a large community you can add crystalline B12 to a mass-produced staple food that everyone eats, such as soymilk. In a small community or family, it is more practical to take a 25 mcg. tab twice a week. The body stores extra B12 in the liver (the only B vitamin stored for more than days or weeks), but only absorbs a few micrograms at a time. You cannot get too much, but if you take a lot at a time orally, it won't all get absorbed.

If you use dairy products, ignore this whole page.

about B₁₂

Prenatal Nutrition

While you're pregnant, you will need a well-rounded diet with about 30% more protein and vitamins than before you were pregnant. You will need to eat lots of fresh vegetables, especially dark leafy greens. Although your metabolism increases during pregnancy, you don't need to increase your calories too much, because pregnant women are somewhat less active than non-pregnant women, and it comes out about even. An increase of about 200-300 calories a day, mostly in the latter half of pregnancy, will suffice.

You should drink a lot—about three quarts of liquid a day. This will help you avoid constipation and keep your body flushed out, since your body is working harder than usual growing a baby.

Supplementary Vitamins and Minerals—It is a good idea to take prenatal vitamins and minerals to make good and sure there are enough vitamins and minerals for both you and the baby. Building a baby from the ground up and nourishing the baby day by day increases your need for these nutrients. Even if you conscientiously try to eat all your dark leafy greens and grains and nutritional yeast, it feels good to be sure. Prenatal vitamins differ from regular multi-vitamins in that they contain extra amounts of all the vitamins and minerals that you need for both of you, and a generous amount of iron. Speaking of iron . . .

Iron—You should take one to three iron pills a day (ferrous sulfate or ferrous gluconate, 5 grains) depending on your iron-level blood tests. If your blood is not checked for iron regularly, you should take one tablet three times a day (three tablets). If you take iron with meals, it is easier on your stomach.

Calcium—Pregnant ladies in their last half of pregnancy, and nursing mothers, need to add about 1 gram (15 grains) of calcium carbonate, calcium gluconate or dicalcium phosphate to their diet each day. The most readily absorbed form of calcium is calcium carbonate, next is calcium gluconate. If you take calcium lactate, you will need about twice as much—2 grams.

Protein—You can get plenty of protein in your pregnancy by eating daily a cup of soybeans and drinking a cup and a half of soymilk or soy yogurt, or by eating half a pound (about a cup) of tofu and drinking a pint of soymilk or soy yogurt, or by eating a cup of hydrated TVP and drinking a quart of soymilk or soy yogurt, or by drinking a quart of soymilk or soy yogurt and eating half a cup of soybeans. If you eat dairy products as well, you should get enough protein from eating daily two cups of cottage cheese, or drinking a quart of milk, yogurt, or buttermilk and eating half a cup of cottage cheese. If you have a little morning sickness, try soy yogurt, soymilk and tofu. They are very mild on the stomach.

Other protein foods include beans and grains eaten together and peanut butter sandwiches.

FEEDING YOUR BABY

Breast Milk—When you are fully nursing with no solid supplement, you give your baby about 800-1000 ml. of milk a day (about one quart). This milk provides everything baby needs for the first 6-8 months if you are well-nourished yourself. You should continue taking pre-natal vitamins and 1 gram of calcium daily throughout nursing to make sure there are plenty of vitamins and minerals for you and your milk.

Breastmilk is very healthful for baby because it contains white blood cells, antibodies, and other substances which destroy germs.

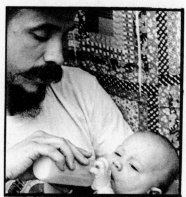

Formula—If you must give baby a formula, look on the labels and find a brand that contains 1.5% protein (with 60% lactalbumin and 40% casein), 7% carbohydrate (lactose), and is fortified with iron and vitamin D. Never give a young baby straight cow's milk or straight soymilk, because it contains too much protein for baby's system to handle.

If you need to give a bottle because you are working, you could consider pumping or hand-expressing some of your milk to be refrigerated and given while you are away.

Vitamin D—The best source of vitamin D is sunlight. Sunlight reacts with oils in the skin to form vitamin D. If you live in a relatively sunless situation such as a northern or cloudy country or a city with a lot of pollution, you will need to supplement vitamin D. You can give vitamin drops which contain vitamins D, A and C. Vitamin D is important for preventing rickets, a condition found in northern or cloudy countries or in children in big city tenements who don't see the sun. Rickets is not found in the more tropical latitudes except in unusual circumstances, such as totally occlusive clothing.

Vitamin D is stored in the body, so a lot of sun on the skin in the summer can last through the winter.

Food—It is best to avoid supplemental feeding for the first 4 months. Baby's digestive system cannot always handle foreign protein or complex starches before this time. Your milk has all the nutrients baby needs for the first 6-8 months, *with the exception of vitamin D.*

If you want to feed baby before 4 months, give only processed baby pablum and/or applesauce. If given too early, proteins and some fruits such as oranges and strawberries can cause food intolerance. **Also, keep in mind that the more food you feed, the less breastmilk is consumed, and therefore less high-quality milk nutrients are consumed.**

Strained Fruits, Vegetables, and Processed Pablum can be introduced at 4-6 months. (But you don't need to until 6-8 months if you don't want to.) Introduce one food at a time and wait several days to see how it is tolerated. Start with applesauce and bananas and rice cereal. Gradually introduce other strained fruits and vegetables. Don't give orange juice until 6 months and don't give strawberries until one year.

Starches and Unprocessed Grains can be introduced at 6-8 months. Mashed cooked grains are different from processed baby cereal (pablum) and are harder to digest.

Thin the strained rice or potatoes with extra liquid at first. For oatmeal, use the instant de-hulled kind. At 6-8 months, babies like to gum toast, cookies, or crackers. Watch them carefully when they start eating these foods until they learn to gum, chew and swallow right. Plain bread is not as good as toast because babies can choke on it until they really have the hang of it. So begin on toast and teething cookies.

Soymilk, Soymilk Yogurt, and Tofu (Bean Curd) can be introduced at 7-8 months. Sterilize the soymilk as you would cow's milk until baby is a year old. You can give your baby soymilk yogurt at this age, too.

Tofu is a good milk protein food for baby. Blend it up or put it through a strainer until he can gum the soft curd unassisted. Tofu is twice as concentrated in protein and other nutrients as soymilk. Give lots of water when you start soymilk or soymilk products (or whole cow's milk).

Nutritional Yeast can be sprinkled on baby's food after 8 months. It is an excellent source of B vitamins, and most brands add B12.

Legumes—You can start trying baby out on beans at 8-9 months. Thin split pea soup is a good one to start with. Any beans you feed your baby must be cooked until *very* soft, skinned, and put through a sieve, blender, or baby food grinder. Add liquid to the mashed beans to make them a soupy consistency rather than a thick paste. Try one kind of bean at a time so you can see which agrees. You can tell whether or not baby is digesting his beans by checking his poop. If the beans come through mostly unchanged or if it smells sour, they aren't being digested. If this happens, stop the beans and give your baby breastmilk, yogurt, and a bland diet for a day or so. Try the beans again now and then, but it is okay if baby can't handle them for a while. You can try soybeans, but they must be *very, very soft,* skinned (remove skins after cooking, or rub the uncooked beans together under water till the skins all come off), and mashed or sieved till smooth. If they are at all crunchy, they will cause diarrhea and a sore red bottom. If they are well-cooked, soybeans do well with most babies. Be sure to add some liquid to the strained or blended soybeans, and be sure to skin them until baby tolerates them really well. Then you can mash them with the skins on.

If baby cannot handle soybeans, don't worry. Some children can't eat them until they are 2-3 years old. The soymilk products and/or "high-protein" baby cereal can cover a child's protein needs indefinitely. High-protein cereal contains enough protein in 1½ cups to meet a child's daily protein requirement through age 3.

Vitamin B12—Baby will get vitamin B12 from your milk as long as he is nursing a lot. Make sure you have a good source of B12 so your milk has it. Your prenatal vitamins probably contain plenty. When baby is weaned or weaning, he will need to be supplemented with B12 just like vegetarian children and adults.

Don't give baby honey before one year of age. There is evidence that honey can contain botulism spores.*

Water—If baby is totally breastfed and you nurse often, additional water isn't necessary. If you give a formula and/or additional food, you must give baby lots of water. Sterilize water until baby is 9-12 months old.

*Reported by the Bacterial Diseases Division, Bureau of Epidemiology, Center for Disease Control.

Feeding Your Young Vegetarian Child

Usually, by one year of age, your child is eating most grown-up food, chopped finely, three meals a day plus snacks. The main nutrient you need to be aware of for the vegetarian child is protein. Soybeans and soy products are the main protein source in the Farm's high-protein vegetarian diet, and these foods need to be steadily worked into your toddler's diet.

Most children can handle soy--milk, soymilk yogurt, and tofu (bean curd) by the time they are 7-8 months old, and de-skinned (either remove skins after cooking, rub skins off under hot water before cooking, or strain through a fine sieve), mashed or blendered soybeans by 8-10 months. If your child can handle it, he should be given soy products every day—a glass of soymilk, raw or lightly cooked tofu, mashed soybeans in a bowl, soy yogurt, soyburgers, or mashed soybeans rolled up in a soft tortilla (our kids' favorite).

The Recommended Daily Allowance for protein for 1-3 year olds is 24 grams a day. About ⅔ of this should come from soy. The remaining ⅓ will come from combinations of grains and vegetables in the rest of the diet. One cup of whole soybeans, or ⅔ cup of mashed soybeans, contains 22 grams of protein.

There are some children who can tolerate soymilk products but not soybeans themselves. They will outgrow this in time, usually by 2-2½ years. Meanwhile, there are other sources of protein. If your child can handle the soymilk products but not the beans, 3 cups of soymilk a day will give 24 grams of protein. Yogurt is the same, and tofu is twice as concentrated as soymilk, so half the amount would provide the recommended daily requirement. If you give him soybeans or some of these soymilk products every day, and a balanced variety of grains, vegetables and fruits, he will be very well nourished.

If your child cannot handle soymilk, try soymilk yogurt and tofu. If they don't work either, give her "high protein" baby cereal (the commercially packaged kind). The soy in this cereal has been processed so that it is very easily digested. 1½ cups of the dry high-protein cereal will provide 20 grams of protein.

You can also make the *High-Protein Soy Bread* on page 174. This bread will have about 7 grams of protein per slice and makes excellent sandwiches or toast.

Peanut butter sandwiches are also a good source of protein for toddlers. It is important to eat the peanut butter with a grain such as bread or crackers because peanuts (or beans) eaten with grains each make the protein of the other more complete and usable.

Other legumes are a good source of protein when eaten with a grain at the same meal. Three-fourths cup of pinto bean or kidney bean chili with two slices of bread will provide about 17 grams of protein (24 grams if you use soy bread). There is a little protein in most vegetables, breads, root vegetables,  etc. So, a well-rounded diet with soy (or soy cereal) as its center will provide quite a bit of protein when you count it up.

If your young child doesn't eat well, try feeding him with other children with good appetites. Don't force him. If you don't feel a kid is eating enough vegetables for vitamins, give chewable kid vitamins until tastes change and mature—they will. Some vegetarian children are anemic (as are many other children) because they don't eat enough beans, iron-containing vegetables, or iron-fortified cereals. If your child is a picky eater and seems pale, tired, and/or irritable, check his blood hematocrit (especially if he is between 9 and 24 months old). This test for anemia is a good check on his nutritional state. If he is anemic, give him kid vitamins with iron.

And don't forget the value of the potato. If eaten in quantity (and most children really like it), the potato has lots of B vitamins and a good amount of vitamin C, as well as minerals and the calories children need. If there are many hours between meals, give your child snacks such as soymilk, raw vegetables, fruit, cookies, or crackers.

Vitamin D

If you live in a northern latitude or in a sunless or cloudy situation, you will need to give your child a vitamin D supplement or a multivitamin containing 400 IU of vitamin D. If you live in a southern latitude, and your child's skin is exposed to the sun, the oils in the skin will react with the sunlight and synthesize vitamin D.

Vitamin B12

If you are feeding your child a totally vegetarian diet— that is, no dairy products or eggs—you will need to give a B12 supplement. You can use a commercial food yeast which has already been fortified with B12, or any other prepared food that is already supplemented (check labels). If you don't use a fortified food, give your child a 10 mcg. or a 25 mcg. (sometimes 10's aren't available) tab of B12, crushed in food, three times a week.

INDEX

INDEX